FORTRESS AMERICA

FORTRESS AMERICA

Gated Communities in the United States

Edward J. Blakely
and
Mary Gail Snyder

Brookings Institution Press
Washington, D.C.

Lincoln Institute of Land Policy
Cambridge, Massachusetts

Copyright © 1997 The Brookings Institution
1775 Massachusetts Avenue, N.W.
Washington, D.C. 20036

and

Lincoln Institute of Land Policy
113 Brattle Street
Cambridge, Massachusetts 02138

Library of Congress Cataloging-in-Publication Data

Blakely, Edward James, 1938–
    Fortress America : gated communities in the United States / Edward J. Blakely and
Mary Gail Snyder.
      p.   cm.
    Includes bibliographical references and index.
    ISBN 0-8157-1002-X (cloth)
1. Gated communities—United States. 2. Community life—United States. I. Snyder,
    Mary Gail. II. Title.
    HT 169.59.U6B53   1997
    307.76—dc21   97-21231
                                                                        CIP

9 8 7 6 5 4 3 2 1

The paper used in this publication meets the minimum requirements of the American National Standard for Information Sciences—Permanence of Paper for Printed
Library Materials, ANSI Z39.48-1984.

Typeset in Times

Composition by Cynthia Stock
Silver Spring, Maryland

Illustration on chapter opening pages by Tom Parsons
Springfield, Virginia

Printed by R. R. Donnelley & Sons Co.
Harrisonburg, Virginia

The Brookings Institution

The Brookings Institution is a private nonprofit organization devoted to nonpartisan research, education, and publication in economics, government, foreign policy, and the social sciences generally. Its principal purposes are to aid in the developent of sound public policies and to promote public understanding of issues of national importance. The Institution was founded on December 8, 1927, to merge the activities of the Institute for Government Research, founded in 1916, the Institute of Economics, founded in 1922, and the Robert Brookings Graduate School of Economics and Government, founded in 1924.

The Institution maintains a position of neutrality on issues of public policy to safeguard the intellectual freedom of the staff. Interpretations or conclusions in Brookings publications should be understood to be solely those of the authors.

Lincoln Institute of Land Policy

The Lincoln Institute of Land Policy is a nonprofit and tax-exempt educational institution established in 1974. Its mission as a school is to study and teach land policy, including land economics and land taxation. The Institute is supported by the Lincoln Foundation, established in 1947 by John C. Lincoln, a Cleveland industrialist. Mr. Lincoln drew inspiration from the ideas of Henry George, the nineteenth-century American political economist and social philosopher.

By supporting multidisciplinary research, educational and publications programs, the Institute brings together diverse viewpoints to expand the body of useful knowledge in three key areas: land use and regulation, taxation of land and buildings, and land values and property rights. Our goal is to make that knowledge comprehesible and accessible to citizens, policymakers and scholars, to improve public and private decisionmaking.

Preface

Gated communities have attracted much attention from the media and generated much controversy. For those who live behind the walls and those who oppose the walls, the topic of gated communities is a troubling issue. For residents of gated communities, the current state of urban America justifies their selecting a neighborhood for the security it provides; for opponents of gated communities, sealing off neighborhoods and creating walled enclaves further fragments our fragile social and economic fabric.

Gated communities are not merely another form of residential settlement. They are part of a deeper social transformation. In many respects, the gates are a metaphor for the social processes at work in the nation's political and social landscape. As with many social issues—immigration, affirmative action, abortion—the debate over gating will not be settled by a book, an article, or piles of data. This book reflects on the broad issues that gating represents. It sharpens the focus on complex issues: private versus public rights and responsibilities, and the practice of community.

This book is about gated communities and their residents—what they want, why they choose gates, and what their lives are like behind them. It is also about community and how gating reflects national social goals, norms, and mores. The questions we explore relate to the practice of community in gated areas, the civic and social bonds that people form both inside the gates and beyond them. We discuss security, crime, privatization, and economic and social segregation as a context for understanding how Americans are seeking social cohesion in turbulent times.

This book is intended for public officials, policymakers, educators, and the general public—people who live in gated communities, people who live outside them, and people interested in the ways we choose to construct our communities and our society. In presenting the perspectives of residents, opponents, developers, and public officials, this book is intended to open serious discussion and discourse. Most important, it presents a set of policy issues with which the nation must come to grips.

People across the nation face difficult decisions when choosing settlement systems that alter not only the appearance but also the character of community. These issues are not easy to resolve, and public policy on the shape of our neighborhoods and cities cannot be left to chance. Every city or town that makes a decision about this matter makes a small but important decision about the entire national social fabric. Any decision citizens make about the form of community settlement ultimately affects the character of that community and of the nation as a whole.

This book would not have been possible without the financial support of the Lincoln Institute of Land Policy of Cambridge, Massachusetts, and the John H. Simon Guggenheim Memorial Foundation. Among the staff at the Lincoln Institute, we would like to thank Deborah Miness and Rosalind Greenstein, who shepherded the project in its research phase. We especially thank Alice Ingerson, director of publications, for her support and invaluable comments.

The Lincoln Institute also sponsored a one-day meeting in Cambridge, where we received many helpful comments and suggestions at an early stage in the project. Our thanks to the participants in that meeting: Ben Chinitz, Lincoln Institute; David Dillon, *Dallas Morning News*; Robert Einsweiler, Lincoln Institute; Ellie Lang, First American Title Company; Sylvia Lewis, American Planning Association; Gary Pivo, University of Washington; Lynn Sedway, Sedway and Associates; David

Sewicki, Georgia Tech; Gerda Wekerle, York University; and James Winokur, University of Denver. We also extend our appreciation and gratitude to Anthony Downs of the Brookings Institution and to three anonymous reviewers, all of whom carefully read the manuscript and provided valuable comments that shaped the final form of the book.

We are also in debt to the members of the fourth estate. Newspaper reporters were an invaluable source of information. Their leads and reports got us started by telling us where gated communities exist and about some of the social and economic issues in those localities. We cannot name them all, but we are very grateful to literally hundreds of journalists and their editors.

For help in organizing site visits in various cities, we thank Ellie Lang, Sergio Ramirez, Rick Szymanski, Fran Toscano, John Tuitte, Frank Turner, and Paul Waddell. Jim King of Applied Development Economics (ADE) in Sacramento, California, facilitated our focus group discussions and gave us the benefit of his insights. Our thanks also to the staff at the Institute of Urban and Regional Development at the University of California at Berkeley, including Christine Amado, Martha Conway, and Miho Rahm, and especially manager Barbara Hadenfeldt, who read and commented on drafts of the manuscript. Wende Green and Ellie Tostado, administrative assistants to Ed Blakely at the University of Southern California, were continuously helpful in countless ways. We are also grateful for Brookings' editorial assistance: Nancy Davidson, Janet Mowery (editing), Inge Lockwood (proofreading), Kurt Lindblom (verification), and Deborah Patton (indexing).

Finally, during site visits and in focus group sessions across the country, hundreds of people provided us with their time and viewpoints. Most must remain anonymous, but we extend our thanks to all.

Contents

1. Forting Up   1

2. The Search for Community   29

3. Gates to Paradise: Lifestyle Communities   46

4. I Have a Dream: The Prestige Communities   74

5. Enclaves of Fear: Security Zone Communities   99

6. You Can Run, But You Can't Hide   125

7. Not-So-Brave New World   144

8. Building Better Communities   161

Appendix   178

Notes   180

References   194

Index   203

1

Forting Up

THE SETTING of boundaries is always a political act. Boundaries determine membership: someone must be inside and someone outside. Boundaries also create and delineate space to facilitate the activities and purposes of political, economic, and social life. Using physical space to create social place is a long and deep American tradition.

Gated communities, one of the more dramatic forms of residential boundaries, have been springing up around the country since the early 1980s. Millions of Americans have chosen to live in walled and fenced communal residential space that was previously integrated with the larger shared civic space. Civic space is more than a political or jurisdictional construct. It is a manifestation of society, culture, and the shared polity.

In this era of dramatic demographic, economic and social change, there is a growing fear about the future in America. Many feel vulnerable, unsure of their place and the stability of their neighborhoods in the face of rapid change. This is reflected in an increasing fear of crime that is unrelated to actual crime trends or locations, and in the growing number of methods used to control the physical environment for physical and economic security. The phenomenon of walled cities and gated communities is a dramatic manifestation of a new fortress mentality growing in America. Gates, fences, and private security guards, like exclusionary land-use policies, development regulations, and an assortment of other planning tools, are means of control, used to restrict or limit access to residential, commercial, and public spaces.

Americans are electing to live behind walls with active security mechanisms to prevent intrusion into their private domains. Americans of all classes are forting up, attempting to secure the value of their houses, reduce or escape from the impact of crime, and find neighbors who share their sense of the good life. The new fortress developments are predominantly suburban, with a growing number of urban inner-city counterparts. They are, however, more than walled-off areas and refuges from urban violence and a rapidly changing society. They are also a search for sociospatial community—the ideal community that Americans have sought since the landing of the Pilgrims.

Gated communities are residential areas with restricted access in which normally public spaces are privatized. They are security developments with designated perimeters, usually walls or fences, and controlled entrances that are intended to prevent penetration by nonresidents. They include new developments and older areas retrofitted with gates and fences, and they are found from the inner cities to the exurbs and from the richest neighborhoods to the poorest. Their gates range from elaborate two-story guardhouses staffed twenty-four hours a day to roll-back wrought-iron gates to simple electronic arms. Guardhouses are usually built with one lane for guests and visitors and a second lane for residents, who may open the gates with an electronic card, a code, or a remote control device. Some communities with round-the-clock security require all cars to pass the guard, issuing identification stickers for residents' cars. Others use video cameras to record the license plate numbers and sometimes the faces of all who pass through. Entrances without guards have intercom systems, some with video monitors, that residents may use to screen visitors.

The residences we are discussing are not multi-unit, high-density apartment and condominium buildings with security systems or doormen in which gates or guards prevent public access to lobbies, hallways, and parking lots. Gated communities are different: their walls and fences preclude public access to streets, sidewalks, parks, beaches, rivers, trails, playgrounds—all resources that without gates or walls would be open and shared by all the citizens of a locality.

We estimate that more than 3 million American households have already sought out this new refuge from the problems of urbanization.[1] In 1985 gated communities existed in only a handful of places. Today they can be found in every major metropolitan area. These developments in part reflect the notion of community as an island, a social bulwark against the general degradation of the urban social order; they also reflect the increasing attempt to substitute private controls for public organization, for the joint responsibilities of democratic citizenship all of us share. Gates and walls are not necessary or natural consequences of these social trends, or causes of them; they are, rather, a dramatic manifestation of them.

Gates and fences around our neighborhoods represent more than simple physical barriers. Gated communities manifest a number of tensions: between exclusionary aspirations rooted in fear and protection of privilege and the values of civic responsibility; between the trend toward privatization of public services and the ideals of the public good and general welfare; and between the need for personal and community control of the environment and the dangers of making outsiders of fellow citizens.

The gated communities phenomenon has enormous policy consequences. It allows some citizens to secede from public contact, excluding others from sharing in their economic and social privilege. This result raises an ideological question that prompts polarized viewpoints. Are gated communities a metaphor of the exclusionary fortress, creating walls between citizens, or are they refuges from the forces that threaten family, economic security, and quality of life?

Underlying our study is the question of how gated communities reflect community and citizenship in America. The real issue is not about the actual gates and walls, but why so many feel they need them. What is the measure of nationhood when the divisions between neighborhoods require guards and fences to keep out other citizens? When public services and even local government are privatized, when the community of responsibility stops at the subdivision gates, what happens to the function and the very idea of a social and political democracy? Can this nation fulfill its social contract in the absence of social contact?

The Evolution of Gated Communities

Gated and walled cities are as old as city-building itself. In England the earliest gated communities were built by the occupying Romans around

300 B.C. Roman soldiers were given land and estates in tribal areas after their term of service in the army in order to buttress and stabilize Roman order in the vast and sparsely defended countryside. Roman families clustered near or within the manor precinct and erected walls and other defenses. Contrary to popular belief, the walls around these settlements were seldom to protect against external invaders but rather to guard against the local villagers who might turn on the baron at any moment. Tribespeople often rebelled against their masters for real and imagined grievances. Later, fortresses also served to protect against invaders or internal warring factions.

Thus the systems of walls and class division was deeply ingrained in England. Successive kings Henry I, Richard II, and Charles II holed up in the Tower of London to protect themselves against either rebellious nobles or hostile and dangerous villagers. London had no police force until the eighteenth century, so people of means forted up to protect themselves and their clans from the savagery of the local population. The heritage of this system can still be seen on the English landscape in the walled abbeys, manors, and castles.[2]

Walled and gated military settlements were also built in the New World, with the earliest being the Spanish fort towns in the Caribbean. Not until the latter half of the nineteenth century did the first purely residential gated neighborhoods appear. Upper-income gated developments like New York's Tuxedo Park and the private streets of St. Louis were built in the late 1800s by wealthy citizens to insulate themselves from the troublesome aspects of rapidly industrializing cities.[3] During the twentieth century more gated, fenced compounds were built by members of the East Coast and Hollywood aristocracies for privacy, protection, and prestige. But these early gated preserves were different from the gated subdivisions of today. They were uncommon places for uncommon people.

Gated communities remained rarities until the advent of the master-planned retirement developments of the late 1960s and 1970s. Retirement developments like Leisure World were the first places where average Americans could wall themselves off. Gates soon spread to resorts and country club developments, and then to middle-class suburban subdivisions. In the 1980s, upscale real estate speculation and the trend to conspicuous consumption saw the proliferation of gated communities around golf courses that were designed for exclusivity, prestige, and leisure.

English abbey wall

The decade also marked the emergence of gated communities built primarily out of fear, as the public became increasingly preoccupied with violent crime. Gates became available in developments of suburban single-family tracts and high-density urban apartment complexes. Since the late 1980s, gates have become ubiquitous in many areas of the country; there are now entire incorporated cities that feature guarded entrances.

Because gated communities in their contemporary form first began in resort and retirement areas, they are most common in the Sunbelt states of the Southeast and Southwest. Thereafter they began to appear in metropolitan areas in all parts of the country. They came later to the Northeast, Midwest, and Northwest, where the trend toward gating is now growing rapidly. In absolute numbers, California and Florida are home to the most gated communities, with Texas running a distant third. Gated communities are also common around New York City, Chicago, and other major metropolitan areas, but they are found nearly everywhere—in Oregon, Washington, Iowa, Minnesota, Wisconsin, Pennsylvania, Arkansas, Massachusetts, Hawaii, Kansas, Missouri, Michigan, Nevada, and the District of Columbia suburbs of Virginia and Maryland. Because they are primarily a phenomenon of metropolitan agglomerations, they are rare in largely rural states like the Dakotas, Vermont, and West Virginia (see figure 1-1).

Figure 1-1. *Gated Community Concentrations*

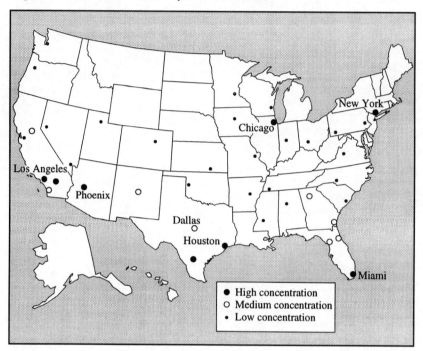

● High concentration
○ Medium concentration
• Low concentration

Martha Conway, Institute of Urban and Regional Development, University of California at Berkeley.

Although early gated communities were restricted to retirement villages and compounds for the super rich, the majority of the newer settlements of the 1970s to 1990s are middle to upper-middle class. Higher-end tracts in planned communities are now commonly gated. Gates are more common in larger tracts because there are more units over which to spread the cost of walling, gating, and constructing and staffing guardhouses. For similar reasons, they also are more common in townhouse and other higher-density developments, where unit costs are often low enough to place gates within the reach of the middle class. However, gates are not yet commonplace for the lower end of the income spectrum, even in California. We estimate that one-third of the developments built with gates are luxury developments for the upper and upper-middle class, and perhaps another third are retirement oriented (see figure 1-2). The remainder are mostly for the middle class, although there are a growing number of working-class gated communities.

Figure 1-2. *The Increase in Gated Communities, 1870–2000*

Number of units

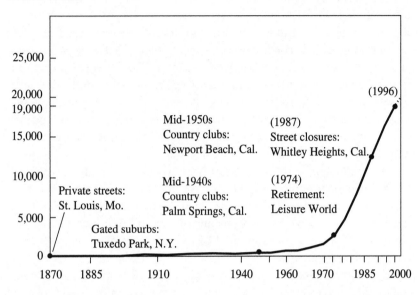

Christine Amado, Institute of Urban and Regional Development, University of California at Berkeley.

We estimate in 1997 that there are as many as 20,000 gated communities, with more than 3 million units.[4] They are increasing rapidly in number, in all regions and price classes. A leading national real estate developer estimates that eight out of every ten new urban projects are gated.[5] Suburban fortified developments are also proliferating. In 1988 one-third of the 140 projects in development in Orange County, California, were gated, double the proportion just five years earlier. In 1989 a construction company in the area reported three times the demand for gated communities as for nongated communities.[6] In the nearby San Fernando Valley, there were approximately a hundred gated communities in existence by the end of the 1980s, nearly all built since 1979.[7] A 1990 survey of southern California home shoppers found that 54 percent wanted a home in a gated, walled development; the question had not even been asked a handful of years earlier.[8] On Long Island, gated communities were rare in the mid-1980s, but by the mid-1990s they had become common, with a gatehouse included in almost every condominium development of more than fifty units.[9] Chicago, suburban Atlanta, and nearly all other large U.S. cities report similar trends.[10]

Economic and social segregation are not new. In fact, zoning and city planning were designed, in part, to preserve the position of the privileged with subtle variances in building and density codes. But gated communities go further in several respects than other means of exclusion. They create physical barriers to access. They also privatize community space, not merely individual space. Many gated areas also privatize civic responsibilities like police protection and communal services such as street maintenance, recreation, and entertainment. The new developments can create a private world that need share little with its neighbors or with the larger political system.

The first step in creating this private world is controlling access to it. From the beginning, the suburbs have intended to separate their residents, first from the city and later even from each other. Over time, developers have devised many means of controlling access. Street design was the original and favored technique for providing exclusivity and privacy in the suburbs. Michael Southworth has documented how developers progressively sealed off suburban residential areas by altering the old grid street patterns, moving from the gridiron to interrupted parallels, to loops and lollipops.[11] These street patterns thwarted easy automobile access and created successively more self-contained, self-focused, and unconnected subdivisions that made it easier for residents to control their own space. The move away from the grid was an intentional device, similar to the gate today. Convoluted dead-end streets limit access and restrict who enters the area by acting as a deterrent to all nonresidents—casual visitors as well as criminals (see figure 1-3).

Many other forms of control of access and space, less tangible than street design, have been developed over the decades. These have included single-use zoning and inaccessibility to public transit. As the suburban form developed, one of the most important changes besides street patterns was that public buildings and public spaces no longer anchored the center of a town. The new, solely residential developments were designed to focus inward, emphasizing private over public space. Private backyards and fenced-in areas shielded neighbors from one another. The carport or garage replaced the porch in the front of the house, reorienting the dwelling unit to its rear, away from the street, neighbors, and other people. With the decline of public space, increasingly sophis-

Figure 1-3. *Street Patterns: Urban Grid to Suburbs*

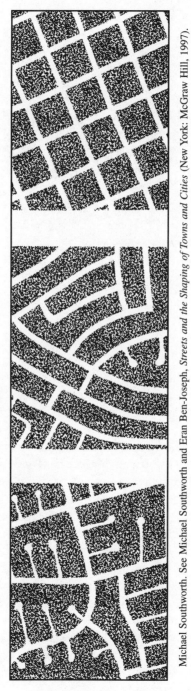

Michael Southworth. See Michael Southworth and Eran Ben-Joseph, *Streets and the Shaping of Towns and Cities* (New York: McGraw Hill, 1997).

A typical gate

ticated and complete private subdivision amenities emerged as a replacement for the common street front and easy communications across porches and front yards. Gating of this inwardly focused residential space became a natural and almost predictable development along the continuum of ever-reduced inter- and intra-communal communications.

Today gates and walls, much more hard and fixed barriers than street patterns, control entrance and egress in suburban subdivisions and urban neighborhoods around the country. Along with the trend toward gating in the suburbs, city neighborhoods are also using barricades and gates with increasing frequency. In neighborhoods built on the old grid pattern, street closures attempt to simulate the suburban pattern by altering access. It is there, in the older neighborhoods retrofitted with gates, that we see the intention behind gates most clearly, much more clearly than in pristine new subdivisions built with guardhouses. Gates are a more intense and obvious method of controlling access than the older, more subtle suburban designs, but they are not an entirely new phenomenon. They are the outgrowth of decades of suburban design and public land-use policy. Gates are firmly within the suburban tradition: they

A barricaded inner-city street in Los Angeles

enhance and harden the suburbanness of the suburbs, and they attempt to suburbanize the city.

The Suburbs as Utopias

Gated communities are part of the trend of suburbanization, and their roots lie in the same urban design tradition. The suburb is a distinctly American form, but its roots can be traced to nineteenth-century England. The artificial village features we find in planned unit developments are vestiges of the development of English country homes in the industrial era. Emulating the landed country gentry, merchants and industrialists built small country estates in or on the fringe of remote villages that lay along the new paved highways developed during the reign of George III.[12] Those same towns received the first rails as well. Over time, more rapid transportation opened country living to people with money, not merely those with landed wealth and inherited social position.[13]

In the United States, a similar pattern of transportation improvements spelled the end of the walking city and fostered the growth of the suburbs.[14] And while the associations of peerage disappeared in the New World, the trappings of class and status remained. Only prosperous, established citizens could afford to commute to the city. The earliest developer-planned suburb, New Brighton on Long Island, offered what suburban developers still advertise: "the means of withdrawing from the labor and anxiety of commerce to the quiet of their own families."[15]

Suburbs are not a recent innovation of market-driven developers. They have a long utopian history of famous designers and visionaries attempting to create the good life and the good society. Intentional community design can be traced back to Robert Owens in the late eighteenth century. Owens and his French contemporary Charles Fourier were among the first in the Western tradition to suggest that the place-form could affect human emotions and influence social systems: "The ideas informing the communal life style—perfectibility, order, brotherhood, merging of mind and body, experimentation, and the community's uniqueness—all represent its intentional quality, with harmony as their principal theme: harmony with nature, harmony among people, and harmony between spirit and the flesh."[16]

Later, in the nineteenth century, designers such as Frederick Law Olmsted and Frank Lloyd Wright created utopian environments around curvilinear streets or cul-de-sacs, building self-contained, separate developments with carefully constructed identities (see figure 1-4).[17] The earliest suburbs offered the same features that attract residents today: quality housing, security, proximity to city amenities, and exclusivity.

No architect had more influence on the American suburban form than Frank Lloyd Wright. His house form—a single-story, servantless dwelling of grace and elegance—created the archetype for the suburban home and made it the preferred and envied housing type of middle-class America. Frank Lloyd Wright designed it, Norman Rockwell articulated it, and the movies and television popularized and glamorized it. This style of housing allowed middle-class mobility with comfort and efficiency and provided for easy subdivision assembly on a large scale based on a master plan. The Wright suburban form found its way into "modern communities" designed by Olmsted and others in Berkeley,

Figure 1-4. *A Historical Suburban Street Plan: Riverside, Illinois, 1868: Olmsted, Vaux & Co.*

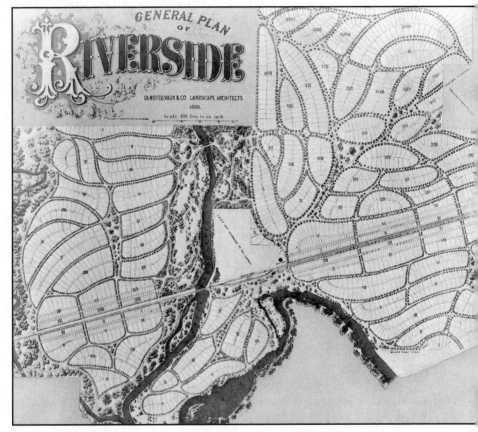

Courtesy of the National Park Service, Frederick Law Olmsted National Historic Site.

California, Tarrytown Heights, New York, and Riverside, Illinois. Their streetcar suburbs were in turn the precursors to the auto suburbs of Levittown and the modern bedroom communities.

The suburb, sign of middle-class rank and position, has been city-averse from its beginning. The English merchant, the American industrialist, and later the middle-class American worker all were trying to escape the city. In the case of the English, the flight to the suburbs was an escape from the unhealthy and uncomfortable dirt and congestion of industrial London. But even as the suburbs might be an escape or a respite, London was still perceived as the action center, and suburban dwellings were second homes, used for weekend and summer retreats. As Samuel Johnson said, "When a man is tired of London, he is tired of life; for there is in London all that life can afford."[18]

The American suburb is very different in character and intention. Unlike its English predecessor, it became the primary residential locus very early in the industrialization process. The American merchant class could not afford two dwellings. Moreover, land in this country was cheap and open space plentiful. Thus, while industrial development spawned urbanization, it also created suburbanization as a component of this process. As early as 1815 a new middle class was emerging and finding its way out of the central cities. Brooklyn Heights, for example, was a suburb away from Manhattan, as were most of the Bronx, Long Island, and Yonkers. By 1911, three years after manufacture of the first mass-produced Ford began, 38 percent of New York's lawyers already lived outside the borough of Manhattan.

The creators of the suburbs did everything they could to dissociate their developments from the city. Names of developments were usually built around words like "park," "forest," "river," "hills," or "valley," mixed with "view," "park," or "estates." The resulting Forest Parks and Green Valley Estates were meant to conjure up bucolic rural imagery and only coincidentally to reflect the actual landscape.

As Kenneth Jackson documents, the flight to the suburbs has been going on for decades, although it has sometimes been masked by aggressive annexation strategies that incorporated suburbs into the city limits.[19] Nowhere is this more clearly manifested than in Los Angeles, where the old city names of Hollywood, San Fernando, Pico, Westwood, and Studio City have more civic identity than the city that annexed them. But the era in which suburbs were incorporated into growing cities is long over, and the physical, social, and economic distinctions between city and suburb are sharper than ever. A majority of Americans now live in suburbs. Driven by lower costs and the desire to avoid low-income minorities (who are equated with crime) and other urban problems, the expansion of the suburbs is likely to accelerate as development moves ever farther out, supported by and leapfrogging beyond the new economic centers of the edge cities.[20]

The suburbs are meant to fulfill a number of aspirations: they should offer close proximity to nature; they should be safe; they should have good education and good kids in the schools; they should shelter residents from social deviance of every form; they should be clean and friendly; they should keep out or limit anything that varies from their physical form and architecture. But suburbs are no longer as uniform or as racially and ethnically sterile as that ideal. Demographic, social, and cultural changes have permeated society, and the suburbs are changing and diversifying. As the suburbs age and become more diverse, they have encountered problems once thought of as urban: crime, vandalism, disinvestment, and blight.

"Suburban" no longer automatically means safe, beautiful, or ideal. The automobile, the rising middle-class minorities of Asians, Hispanics, and African Americans, and equal housing access laws have made it difficult for the white middle class to find refuge in suburban distance alone. And no place is truly safe. If security cannot be found in location alone, perhaps it can be found in a development type—the gated community. And perhaps the much-longed-for community of face-to-face contact in a defined neighborhood territory can also be found behind walls.

Building Dreams, Denying Reality

Gated communities have their antecedents in modern utopias, but they have been transformed into a totally new product, organized and marketed as a solution to contemporary problems rather than as a search for a better communal system. Part of the explanation for the increase in gated communities is the logic of developers, for whom gated communities are a marketing device, another way to target specific submarkets, or, in some areas, a necessity to meet demand.

Developers are often perceived as trend followers. Certainly any developer who saw a competitor using gates successfully would be likely to modify his or her own development strategy to include at least some of the new product. This bandwagon effect means that once gated communities are introduced into an area, their numbers quickly multiply. With their often elaborate guardhouses and entrance architecture, gates also provide the crucial product differentiation—and clear identity—

Advertisement for a gated community stands in the shadow of city hall, Los Angeles.

that is needed in crowded and competitive suburban new home markets. Whenever a significant recreational feature such as a golf course or lake is part of a development, the gate controls access and assures buyers that the amenity will be theirs alone. In addition, many builders report faster sales in gated communities, and quicker turnover can mean substantial additional profit.[21]

There is little agreement among developers as to whether housing behind gates commands a price premium over that in similar nongated communities. Similarly, realtors evince no consensus on whether gates add to a home's price or help to maintain property values. We compared resale prices of comparable gated and nongated housing within a two-mile radius in Orange County, California, the heavily gated coastal suburbs of Los Angeles. We analyzed a small area to isolate the effect of gates from other locational factors such as geographic variations in market performance and amenities such as schools. This area of Orange County also offers a wide range of housing types, a significant percentage of which are gated, allowing for good matching of comparable housing (see figure 1-5).

Over the five-year period from 1991 through 1995, no consistent

Figure 1-5. *Price Comparisons, Gated and Nongated Communities, Orange County, CA, 1991–95*

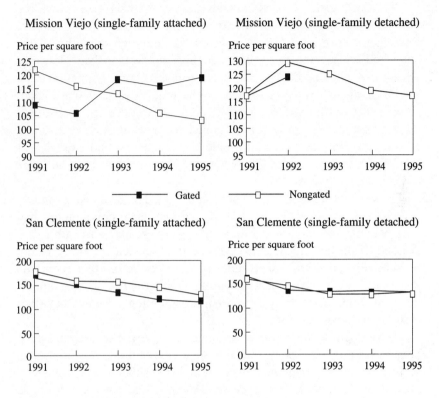

Source: Meyers Company, Orange County, California.

pattern emerges from the sales data. In general, price differences were small, and gated communities even had a slight price disadvantage. Although these data cannot be generalized to all local housing markets, we can conclude that gates do not automatically confer a premium on housing prices. Interestingly, gates did not help maintain property values in a declining market. In only one case—attached single-family homes in Mission Viejo—did gated communities perform better than nongated ones in holding real estate values during a period of declining prices. Just as for developers, for whom faster sales provide clear financial benefit, homeowners gain economic benefits from quicker sale of their properties. Although these data reflect price and not the speed of sales, they indicate that gates cannot be assumed to increase value or to maintain it.

The developers of gated communities see themselves as providing both security and social familiarity, especially to certain submarkets. The elderly have been targets of gated communities since the 1970s, and gated second-home complexes are also well established. Now others are perceived as likely markets for gates, including empty nesters, who are likely to be away on long vacations frequently, and young double-income families, in which no one is home during the day. Security is viewed as freedom, not just from crime but also from such annoyances as solicitors and canvassers, mischievous teenagers, and strangers of any kind, malicious or not. The gates provide sheltered common space not penetrable by outsiders.

This drive for security is, of course, reflected in the housing market. A developer we interviewed in 1994 said that gated communities had only become common in the previous several years as a result of increased violence and decreased municipal services.[22] Many in the homebuilding and real estate industries are predicting that economic insecurity and fear of crime will spur the rapid growth of gated communities and home security systems. People are feeling insecure; they want their home to be a fortress.

Developers do not, however, prominently advertise security or safety, or promise it in their promotional brochures. Even the most high-tech security systems cannot guarantee a crime-free subdivision, and developers fear liability if they make such claims. The gate is part of the design and amenities package that sells houses by selling the image of a life style that buyers wish to identify with. As one developer of gated communities in Florida told us, "Selling houses is showbiz. You go after the emotions. We don't go out and show a gate in the ad. But we try to imply and do it subtly. In our ad, we don't even show houses. We show a yacht. We show an emotion."[23]

Developers use "community" as a term of art to discuss their products in promotional materials. Marketing brochures are written to convey a sense of community, referring to housing tracts as "new communities within a city," "a totally new way of life," "an old community setting," or even "your new hometown." The language is an integral part of the strategy to sell houses. Some developers also believe that gates intensify and highlight the feeling of belonging, the positive emotions we associate with community. A national developer and consultant told us that he believes gates help sell a subdivision by creating the feeling of community: "When you drive home, you would feel that you were home at one of two places: when you turn onto your street or when you turn into your driveway. When I put a gate on an entrance, I can extend that feeling of home, which is so strong in you, it feels unbelievable. I can extend it from as far away as your house is from the gate."[24]

Developers have long been innovators, not just in the design of streets and housing but also in the design of social institutions. Community cannot be achieved by physical design alone. Ebenezer Howard understood this well. In designing his influential Garden City in the nineteenth century, he focused on the system of governance as much as spatial form. He devised a plan to both build and finance his development through an internal organization. His community organizations were to collect rent for public services. The development would be independent of the municipal government, free of the interest politics of local government.[25] Howard wrote in his charter: "In the council (or its nominees) are vested the rights and powers of the community as sole landlord of Garden City. . . . By stepping as a quasi public body into the rights of a private landlord, it becomes at once clothed with far larger powers for carrying out the will of the people than are possessed by other local bodies, and thus solves to a large extent the problems of local self government."[26]

Howard's ideas were adapted by Charles Stern Ascher, a lawyer turned planner. Ascher extended the notion of private government to develop the master-planned suburb of Radburn, New Jersey, in 1928.[27] He was attracted to Ebenezer Howard's ideas of communal private ownership, but he felt the need to further privatize and protect his development by using restrictive covenants. In combining the private government with these restrictive covenants, he created an institution, the modern homeowner association, that is now dominant in new housing development.

In part because of the success of Radburn, the model that it established became the vehicle of choice for large-scale housing builders. Covenants were built into house deeds and imposed such things as minimum housing standards and uniform building lines. They sometimes also barred purchase by nonwhites and Jews. By using restrictive covenants and establishing the homeowner association government to monitor compliance, they could control the long-term quality of their housing developments and so guarantee future prices and gain community support. These developers moved well beyond housing construction to creating a new way of life. The gated community is the newest innovation in a long historical trend to ever more controlled, ever more privatized residential environments.

Governing by Legal Contract, Not Social Contact

One of the more important features of the gated community is not the gate itself but the underlying governance system that it requires. Gated communities are run by self-governing homeowner associations (HOAs).[28] It is a feature they share with private street subdivisions everywhere. In these subdivisions, which are the dominant form of new development nationally, each property owner shares legal ownership of streets, sidewalks, and other common facilities, including gates, with their fellow homeowners. Elected boards oversee this common property, and each home comes bound with covenants, conditions, and restrictions (CC&Rs) as part of the deed. CC&Rs set the rules regarding common property but also regarding individual homes. This degree of control is already impressive in a subdivision without gates; when gates and fences are built around such a development, control reaches an even higher level.

Developers use HOAs for a number of purposes.[29] Homeowner associations help protect property values by ensuring uniformity in the development, and by ensuring that the original standards remain in perpetuity. This protects against changes made not only by individual homeowners but also by local government. The developer appeals to the homeowners' natural instinct to preserve and protect their investments from the unwanted interference of local government—such as zoning changes to allow multiple dwellings, commercial facilities, or group homes. Suburban neighborhoods have been transformed into collectively owned property in part to circumvent government regulation and social responsibility.

Local governments also often favor developments that incorporate homeowner associations, because the developers also pay for new streets, sewers, and other infrastructure, who then pass the cost on to the home purchasers. Maintenance costs are likewise privatized and so removed from strapped municipal budgets. In some states, such as California, the association may collect infrastructure bond taxes through a quasi-governmental apparatus established at the time of development.[30]

The association is a private entity that can make its own rules. These rules are enshrined in the nation's constitutional private property rights. Collective property rights are as unassailable as individual rights and have been upheld by the Supreme Court. As Justice William O. Douglas, a noted liberal, opined: "A quiet place where yards are wide, people few, and motor vehicles restricted are legitimate guidelines in a land use project addressed to family needs. This goal is a permissible one. . . . The police power is not confined to eliminate filth, stench, and unhealthy places. It is ample to lay out zones where family values, youth values, and blessings of quiet seclusion and clean air make a sanctuary for people."[31]

However, homeowner associations are not as communal or democratic as they might sound. In some, each household, not each adult, gets one vote. In others, the number of votes depends on the value of the property. In addition, HOAs come with covenants, conditions, and restrictions that impose rules on an astonishing array of things both inside and outside the home. In some instances, private patrols give tickets for parking or speeding violations within the compound. In more intrusive homeowner associations, there are rules governing home furnishing that can be seen from the windows and the hours after which residents may not socialize outside their own houses.

These examples are extreme, but even the common run of regulations seem excessive to those who are not used to them. Rules on exterior maintenance and design are standard, requiring that landscaping conform to a common plan and that houses or even front doors be painted a limited number of colors. Pets above certain weight limits are sometimes barred, as are people under a specific age. There may be height limits for shrubs and trees, approved flower lists, prescribed designs for fences and decks. Window air conditioners, backyard swing sets, and satellite dishes are commonly banned. Rules usually forbid hanging laundry outside, leaving garage doors open, parking trucks, campers, or commercial vehicles in driveways, and placing trash cans out on the street before a certain hour. Residents may not be aware of all the rules encoded in the CC&Rs before moving in, or may not understand or accept them, resulting in conflicts within the HOA. Figure 1-6 lists some of the problems that HOA boards reported in a recent survey; all are based in rule or policy violations.

Homeowner associations can be very vigilant, and some even accuse them of vigilantism. Neighborhoods, through homeowner associations, are using zoning, housing restrictions, parking restrictions, and neighborhood police as means to control their neighbors' behavior. Although the goal is to reestablish a sense of genuine mutual community, the means they use are sometimes far less communal than controlling.

The attraction of privately governed subdivisions with their homeowner associations and gates should not be surprising. Their rules provide benefits beyond any protection of property values or aesthetics. They ensure that neighbors need not deal with each other in even the smallest disputes if they prefer not to; instead, they can turn to third parties to arbitrate and enforce violations. The rules of the neighborhood are encoded in their deeds; property managers and security companies are often paid to handle infractions; and the courts can be used to evict recalcitrant residents.

In their preference for avoiding social interaction and cooperation, HOA residents do not differ from our society as a whole. More and more, we purchase services that we used to provide for ourselves. We hire nannies and tutors to rear and teach our children, use "homes" to care for elders, let lobbyists speak for us to our representatives. Gradually, starting with daily life and moving on to family life, civic life, social life, and now neighborhood and community life, people are increasingly ceding older forms of social responsibility to professionals. Gated communities are simply a part of this trend.

Micro-Governance and Civic Secession

Because there is no national list of gated communities, and no feasible way to construct one short of a census, we turn to the available data on homeowner associations to give us some indication of their most likely characteristics. Much of the available data derive from surveys of the membership of the Community Associations Institute (CAI), a national organization of homeowner associations.

In 1992 the CAI estimated that there were some 150,000 homeowner associations in the United States. According to the most recent full survey of their membership, the average number of units in HOAs is 291. Most are much smaller, with nearly half having under 150 units,

Figure 1-6. *Selected Problems in Homeowner Associations*

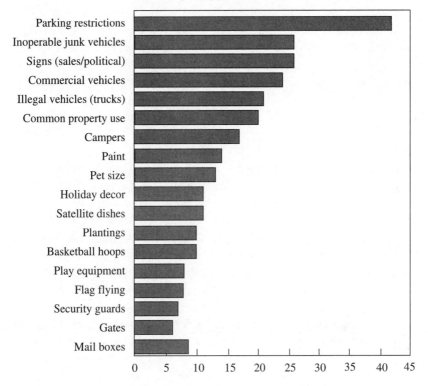

Percent reporting problem

Source: Adapted from Doreen Heisler and Warren Klein, *Inside Look at Community Associa-tion Ownership: Facts and Perceptions* (Alexandria, Va.: Community Association Institute, 1996).

although 11 percent have more than 500 units. About 52 percent are managed by professional management companies; 29 percent are self-managed by volunteers, and 19 percent have on-site managers employed directly by the HOA.[32]

The homeowner associations provide a wide array of services to their residents (see table 1-1). Nearly half include some type of security or crime prevention—gates, fences, guards, or electronic monitoring systems. Other common services include landscaping, garbage pickup, street maintenance, and swimming pools. The majority of these services are provided through contracts with private firms.

The Community Associations Institute has estimated that homeowner associations in the United States are growing at the staggering rate of 10,000 per year.[33] This is a government growth industry. While at the national and state levels the public is asking for less government, at the local level people are creating more governance institutions. These numbers reflect the new privatization of residential government and the rise in business and commercial improvement districts that allow merchant and property owner groups to tax themselves for additional security, parks, and other previously public services. Many observers have questioned whether these private governments constitute an abandonment of the public realm—a "secession of the successful," in the words of Robert Reich.[34]

A number of scholars studying homeowner associations have described homeowner associations as private governments.[35] One legal scholar, David Kennedy, has argued that homeowner associations should be considered "state actors," because the services they perform and the authority they wield within their developments are similar to those of local government.[36] Kennedy notes judicial recognition of roadways, parks and recreation, sanitation, police protection, sidewalks, and streetlights as traditional services provided and maintained by government and cites precedents for the treatment of private agents as state actors when they provide public functions. Under this legal conceptualization, Kennedy argues that the use of gates and barricades to exclude nonmembers from private communities should be viewed as unconstitutional.

These new local pseudo-governments are an attempt to relocalize governance and to avoid public access to local resources. They constitute, as John Petersen says, a powerful force and "generally resist local taxation. They also lobby state legislatures for, among other things, property tax rebates to cover the services they pay for and deliver themselves."[37] New Jersey, Texas, Maryland, and Missouri already allow for adjustments in local taxes to reflect the self-provided services of homeowner associations.[38]

There have always been those who complain about the use of "their" tax money to solve other people's problems, even within the same city or town. The dynamic is an old one, brought to a worrisome new level by its use by these private microgovernments. With the spread of homeowner associations, more and more Americans can set their own taxes in the form of assessments, use them for services they choose, and re-

Table 1-1. *Services Provided by Homeowner Associations*

Service	Providing service
Landscaping	86
Snow removal	84
Garbage pickup	65
Swimming pool	61
Streetlights	58
Street cleaning	57
Clubhouse	38
Tennis	34
Playground	21
Park	16
Basketball	15
Library	12

Source: Doreen Heisler and Warren Klein, *Inside Look at Community Association Home-ownership: Facts and Perceptions* (Alexandria, Va.: Community Associations Institute, 1996), p. 12.

strict those benefits to themselves and their immediate neighbors. From there it is a small step to seceding from a city or county in order to avoid paying for those who don't live in one's HOA.

Civic secession is happening in many places across the country. In California, Florida, and other states with permissive government formation laws, developers are working with residents to create cities that are separate from the existing jurisdiction—city or county. People find these new cities, created by secession, attractive for many reasons. Using housing and growth regulations, the new jurisdictions can pass regulatory ordinances that restrict new entrants. And they can direct publicly collected taxes to locally specific goals rather than allowing them to be used over a larger area.

In California, where it is not difficult to create a new city on unincorporated county land, most of the new secessionary cities follow the Lakewood contract city model. Under the Lakewood scheme, the newly incorporated city contracts with the county government or other municipalities for traditional government services like police, fire, sewer, and water. The new city has to see that services are provided but does not have to provide them itself. In the Lakewood model, the city's role is to be a private association that represents city interests and purchases

A sign at Laguna Sur, Laguna Niguel, California, announces limited access to public areas.

services from private vendors or other local governments—much as homeowner associations already do.

Unhappy with public services and unwilling to contribute to a general pool to pay for services city- or countywide, the residents of some gated communities have seceded from the civic order by incorporating. At least six gated communities are fully independent incorporated cities. Hidden Hills, population 1,812, and Rolling Hills, population 2,076, are both wealthy gated communities outside Los Angeles. Canyon Lake, California, is a mixed-income gated town of 14,000 located in Riverside County east of Los Angeles. Golf, with 114 residents, and Golden Beach, population 612, are near Miami, Florida. Outside Boca Raton, the tiny town of Atlantis put gates and barbed wire–topped walls around its 1,125 homes in the mid-1980s; 70 percent of the city budget goes to pay for the guards and gates.[39] Other developments in California, such as Heritage Ranch in San Luis Obispo County and the 21,000-resident Leisure World in Laguna Hills have considered incorporation. And an existing city, Rosemont, Illinois, outside Chicago, has installed guardhouses, staffed by police, on the public streets leading into its main residential area. Left outside is the commercial area of freeway off-ramp hotels, businesses, and several apartment buildings.[40]

Entrance to Jacaranda Pointe, Plantation, Florida

Incorporation hardens and magnifies the characteristic exclusion, privatization, and secession of many gated communities. The city of Hidden Hills, where white picket fences are mandatory, provides an interesting look at how a town government functions behind walls. The mayor of the neighboring town charges that Hidden Hills does not cooperate or participate with other local governments. For example, when the local mayors hold meetings, Hidden Hills sends only its city clerk. Inside Hidden Hills, a candidate for city office told the *Los Angeles Times* that city politics are "like running for some class office in high school. People tend to vote for those they know or like. There aren't any burning issues."[41]

Control Points

America is an increasingly unequal place. Gated communities are a manifestation of broader social forces unleashed in an unstable metropolitan system. And although gates do not themselves cause inequality or other social problems, they do reflect and illustrate larger patterns and trends in society. The privatization and physical control devices of gated communities attempt to limit, or at least moderate, the influences of the outside world.

In recent years, some authors have linked the rise in gated communities to other architectural and planning innovations: the full-service, enclosed mall; public buildings and public plazas and parks bristling with security mechanisms; cookie-cutter hotels and convention centers; and the skyways and tunnels that allow tourists and downtown workers never to set foot on a city sidewalk.[42] All of these, like gated communities, provide a carefully controlled environment, separate and safe, from which almost anything undesirable can be excluded. Trevor Boddy has described the effect of these new environments as one in which "'being inside becomes a powerful symbol for being protected, buttressed, coddled, while 'being outside' evokes exposure, isolation, and vulnerability."[43] More and more, Americans are turning to protected spaces and away from public space. The rise of gated communities is part of this trend.

2

The Search for Community

THE WORD "community" is often used by developers, public officials, and residents in talking about gated developments. They speak of the practical matters they feel contribute to making a good community: personal and property safety, reduced traffic and noise, and children playing in the streets. They also speak about a feeling of community, or a friendly community, or having neighbors like themselves, where they feel "at home." And nearly all at some point speak about the problems in their neighborhood, in others nearby, or in the world at large. They hope that gates will keep out or reduce these problems.

Many Americans believe that their neighborhoods are under threat, and not just those in the most troubled poverty- and crime-ridden inner-city districts. Crime seems more random, and more vicious. Carjackings and kidnappings occur in peaceful suburbs, the drug trade flourishes even in rural counties, and gangs operate in cities large and small. Youth crime is a major national issue, and the media speak of "superpredators," young teens and even children with no conscience or remorse.

The threat that so many feel also reflects the volatility of their envi-

ronment—increasing diversity, mobility, and changes in family structure—as well as growing income polarization and economic uncertainty.
Rapid changes in these life-influencing factors are themselves seen as a
danger. Uncertainty and instability lead to fear. The home is of central
psychological value, and it represents most families' single largest investment, their most important source of financial security for the future. For the home to be safe, a lock on the door is not enough. The
streets of the neighborhood around it, and the city and region of which it
is part, should also be safe.

Gates, private security guards, and barricades help control one's
environment and improve quality of life. So do Neighborhood Watch,
not-in-my-backyard (NIMBY) movements, neighborhood groups, and
homeowner associations. On a larger scale, the turn to law-and-order
solutions like more police, stiffer sentencing and more jails, and the
replacement of public spaces like plazas and sidewalks with private ones
like malls also represent this search for greater security and control. All
such initiatives are meant to protect against crime by giving the local
residents social and physical control of territory. Some try to gain community empowerment and cohesion by bringing the community together to
make it stronger and better able to ward off threat. Others seek to control people or activities they see as disruptive or destabilizing. Some try
to do both.

Gated communities are part of the trend toward exercising physical
and social means of territorial control. Some walls are meant to keep
people in, some to keep people out. Some are meant to mark territory
and identity, others to exclude. Peter Marcuse has written about different types of walls in cities, from the physical to the social, symbolic,
psychological, and legal. He notes several different purposes to the fences,
gates, walls, and barricades in residential areas. In poor neighborhoods,
gates and barricades may be walls of "protection, cohesion and solidarity," while in gentrified urban neighborhoods, they protect and secure
the advantage of the higher-income newcomers. In the suburbs, they
"exclude for reasons of status and social control, protecting privilege
and wealth from the threat of physical intrusion." [1]

The building of cities and the development of new residential types
often represent in part the search for a better way of life. And always,
one facet of these efforts is the search for community. The residents of
gated communities have varying expectations and motivations, of course.

They want safety and security, and many seek privacy or status. Many hope that the closed, private streets behind gates will lead to a more open, friendly, and cohesive community.

In examining gated communities, we asked how community was affected: what people's expectations were of life behind gates, what experiences they had there, how they participated in neighborhood life, and how they related to the world outside. Did the presence of gates and a perimeter wall affect how residents felt about their neighborhoods, or the way they functioned?

The shape and characteristics of the places we live in have a great influence on our experiences, our social interactions, and our behavior. In this chapter we first explore the issue of community, what it means, and how it is related to the places where we live. Then, after discussing the research design and methodology for this study, we describe the three major types of gated communities and their characteristics.

Defining Community

From Alexis de Tocqueville to contemporary sociologists and policy-makers, our communities and our relationships in them have been seen as key elements of what it means to be American. But what is community?

In the late nineteenth century Ferdinand Tönnies created the duality of gesellschaft and gemeinschaft, which still guides the way we think about community today.[2] Gemeinschaft is "true" community, the natural, emotional, interdependent association among people. Gesellschaft is society, the modern, rational, and instrumental associations we create. Gemeinschaft has become a catch phrase for the old village community, homogeneous, interdependent, and close-knit, and gesellschaft for the impersonal, alienated, mobile, modern society that has replaced it.

In the early decades of this century, the Chicago School of Sociology developed the study of community, and especially neighborhoods, as a way of understanding society. Robert Park and his colleagues viewed the urban neighborhoods of Chicago as communities where residential proximity bred local sentiment and concerned themselves with the social forces that were disrupting neighborhoods and weakening community.[3] They saw the decline of community arising from urbanization and modernization. Increasing mobility, industrialization, the separation of home from work, and the rise of mass culture were seen as attenuating kinship, undermining social solidarity. Secondary social contacts, those based on economic and contractual ties, had become more important than primary social contacts based on kinship, culture, and community.[4]

Later sociologists began to question whether this view of community had been lost in modern times. Gerald Suttles argued that the idea of the decline of community was based in a "golden age" that had never existed. Some theorized that what they saw was not community lost but community transformed. Rather than look for evidence of the ideal gemeinschaft, researchers have looked at the functions that community serves—production, distribution, and consumption of social goods; social control, both formal and informal; socialization; social participation; and mutual support.[5] They find these functions served by communities in many different forms. There is the community of limited liability, where entry and exit are open and follow individual needs;[6] the defended community, defined in opposition to its surroundings;[7] community as the institutions that mediate between the individual and society, like church, family, and neighborhoods.[8] All of these forms may function as communities for their members; all can inspire a "sense of community." Some scholars have identified a "new" kind of community arising in the mobile modern world, one freed of proximity and built on personal links independent of territory.[9] Others measured and quantified these links, seeing modern community as complex and varied networks of primary social ties.[10]

Community is a vague term, loaded with history, moral connotations, nostalgia, and romanticism. And the breadth of work briefly touched on here makes clear that scholars of community have not always been talking about the same thing. Despite this, their definitions do have some commonalities. Community implies sharing: usually a shared territory, certainly shared experiences or social interactions, and also shared traditions, institutions, common goals or purposes, and political or economic structures.[11] It implies not just a feeling of community, but participation in the social life of a place, and often also the political and economic life, because of a sense of shared destiny within the territorial community.

Table 2-1 summarizes several important elements of community. Shared territory is defined by physical or social boundaries. If the boundaries are symbolic or intangible, residents may define their community

Table 2-1. *The Elements of Community*

Element	Function	Examples
Shared territory	Defining the boundaries of the community	Historical names; housing type; subdivision name; walls; gates
Shared values	Defining identity and commonality	Racial/ethnic background; income level/class; religion; history and traditional celebrations
Shared public realm	Common ground for interaction	Public parks; open space; streets and sidewalks; private subdivision facilities
Shared support structures	Mutual aid and association	Voluntary community organizations, charitable and recreational; churches; professional management
Shared destiny	Mechanisms to protect or guide the future	Civic associations; voluntary neighborhood groups; rules and CC&Rs; homeowner associations

differently. Usually physical markers are used—housing type, major roads, or the walls around a gated community. The next element is shared values or the ways in which people define their commonalities with other members of the community and thus construct in part their own identity and that of their community. These may include racial, class, or religious characteristics or common history. All territorial communities also have shared public spaces, where residents can meet and interact. They can be streets and sidewalks, parks, or private country clubs. Shared support structures are the institutions that a community maintains to provide mutual aid and to bring members together in activity. Shared support structures may include churches, charitable organizations, social or recreational clubs like Junior League or Little League; in some HOAs the professional management team is part of the shared support structure. Finally, shared destiny refers to the mechanisms that communities have to protect or guide them. These may include voluntary neighborhood improvement groups, civic associations, or homeowner associations and CC&Rs.

In this book we are dealing with a place-based notion of community, one rooted in the territory of a residential development. Neighborhoods, if they are also communities, consist of more than friends and neighbors living in a set of residences within a collectively identified territory. Neighborhood as community also includes a sense of mutual responsibility, significant interaction, and cooperative spirit.

The concept of community as we use it in this book represents the intensity of common values as expressed by social ties to a place and by the people within it. This notion of community has two facets. The first is the "private" aspect of community, the community of sentiment or "good feelings" that most Americans have in mind when they refer to community. It encompasses feelings of belonging or connection to and identification with a place and its people, and a local culture of mutual support and shared social relationships. The second facet of community is the "public" aspect. This is the community of mutual obligation, shared destiny or goals, direct democracy, and involvement in community affairs. It is a recognition of mutual interdependence, the awareness that the quality of our lives depends on our environment and the people in it. It is more than just living in the same place; and it is more than neighborliness.

Scholars investigating homeowner associations have also looked closely at the idea of community and what the establishment of private mini-governments means for the experience and practice of community. Because gated communities are also developed with homeowner associations, this literature can shed some light on the issue of gates and community. In theory, HOAs would be an excellent vehicle for strong local communities. They have an institutional structure that serves as a pseudo-government and a mechanism for participation and communication. In this sense, HOAs are a form of direct democracy, a means of local control and self-determination that can bring neighbors together in common interest.

In reality this ideal is seldom met. The literature on homeowner associations is full of laments of apathy, conflict, and lack of participation. Studies of homeowner associations have found little evidence that they breed higher levels of participation and self-governance.[12] Robert Dilger attributes this effect to flaws in the structure of HOAs and to the free-rider problem—because participation is voluntary, a few individuals do most of the work, and as long as there are no glaring problems, the majority feel safe leaving those few to bear the burden of running the association.[13]

Carol Silverman and Stephen Barton attribute conflict and lack of participation in HOAs to the dissonance between private property rights and public roles. Residents view HOAs as a means of protecting their private property and guarding against intrusions into the private enjoyment of the home. Because the association is based in these individual goals, rooted in private property rights and ownership, people do not view the obligations of the HOA structure as extending to the public, shared community. Greg Alexander has argued that individuals often simply lack a "participatory consciousness."[14] Alexander views the tensions around community in American life as a conflict between the contractarian and communitarian theories of community. The former, related to rational choice theory, views individuals as atomistic, not connected to each other except as they agree to be connected for personal benefit. In the communitarian ideal, individuals are embedded in society, connected not only through their common humanity but through the social structures they jointly create and benefit from.[15]

Community may be as local as a city block or as large as a region. We may even speak of the national or international community. We are all members of many communities, like a set of concentric circles or overlapping networks. Community is more than a set of local social relationships in America. It is also a political building block and a set of social ideals, formed within a place, a territory. As place and community become commodified, environments we buy into rather than create, our neighborhoods are more and more shaped by economic rather than social institutions. The most recent manifestation of the American urban form moves us away from the old power of place based on relationship to a new power of place based on property ownership. The walls and gates described here are more than obstructions to entry; they are symbols of a new social pattern that may have profound effects on the nation itself.

Research Approach

Scholars have used a broad range of methods to investigate community—its forms, effects, and functions. Studies of individual communities tend to be ethnographic, primarily using participant observation as the central methodology. Urban community research has focused on the ethnic enclave, the ghetto, or the neighborhood. The work of Herbert Gans has been particularly influential in this regard; recently, Elijah Anderson and others have used the technique.[16] Other researchers have augmented participant observation with secondary sources ranging from news reports to statistical data and historical records.

Scholars more interested in social and policy issues than in the sociology of individual communities often employ a methodology that relies primarily on interviews. William Julius Wilson, for example, uses intensive interviews to elicit residents' own stories of community values, goals, and mores; thus he is able to examine socially isolated poor communities, not just the people trapped inside them.[17] Robert Bellah and his colleagues, in their classic study of community, commitment, and individualism in America, *Habits of the Heart*, used interviews with people across the country as the basis for what they called "social science as public philosophy."[18]

The research for this book drew from many of these methodologies. Because gated communities are an emerging phenomenon and scholarly work on them is virtually nonexistent, we approached the research from an investigatory standpoint. We drew from current sources such as newspapers and magazines; we also collected information from residents of gated communities, real estate developers, and public officials as well as citizens' groups and national associations. We began by identifying the physical characteristics and patterns related to the trend toward gated communities, but our primary interest is the social issues surrounding them. Of central concern is the functioning of gated developments as communities, both internally as neighborhoods and externally in relation to the cities, counties, and regions of which they are a part. We have sought to learn what the emergence of gated communities means for our society:

—How do those inside and outside feel about them? Do they perceive gates and walls as meeting the needs of the local population? What opinions do the residents have? The developers? Planners? City government officials?

—What is the gated citizens' experience of community? What degree of community spirit or civic participation do they show within these enclaves? Do they feel a sense of connection and belonging to the people inside the walls, or merely to the place? In what sense are gated communities truly communities?

—What do gated communities imply for the concept of citizenship? How do the residents understand their place within their immediate, and larger, community? Do they feel kinship with the city outside the gates, or only with their walled development? How, and how well, are they connected to the city outside their gates?

We collected both ethno-descriptive data and statistical evidence, integrating site visits and observation, focus groups, interviews, a survey of gated communities, and secondary data sources. Not only are there no national or local statistics on the prevalence or other characteristics of gated communities, likewise, we have found no university, research institute, or trade association that has studied the phenomenon. Consequently, our first step was to identify as many gated communities as possible. First, through on-line searches of full-text newspaper data banks, we identified hundreds of gated communities and began to establish the outlines of the phenomenon.

In tandem with our media searches, we contacted journalists, planners, and other informants who were invaluable in leading us to neighborhood activists, planners, developers, realtors, government officials, trade associations, security consultants and others across the country. From these sources we created a database of the major characteristics of the developments we had identified. After making initial site visits in California, we developed a working typology of gated communities and major themes and issues.

We conducted several focus group sessions and interviews in six metropolitan areas with high concentrations of gated communities: the San Francisco Bay Area; Los Angeles; Riverside–Palm Springs, California; Orange County, California; Dallas; and Miami. The focus group participants were residents of gated communities, public officials, realtors, and developers. The participants in the resident focus groups were chosen to reflect the full range of our typology and were identified from the news media searches and by local informants in academia and journalism. The participants from industry were active in the development or sale of gated communities. The public officials were representatives of planning, fire, and police departments, as well as elected officials involved in setting policy on gating. In some places we also conducted individual interviews to ensure that as many perspectives as possible were included during our short visits to each area.

To ensure that all of the issues were covered and that our preconceptions and biases would not dominate the discussions, an independent facilitator led the focus group sessions. Each session covered a set of general topics as well as a set of specific issues of significance in that locality.

All of the focus group sessions and site visits were in the Sunbelt, the region with the densest concentrations of gated communities. We collected national data through a survey conducted in collaboration with the Community Associations Institute (CAI) in Alexandria, Virginia. The survey was mailed to the boards of approximately 7,000 CAI member associations. About two thousand responses were received, for a response rate of almost 30 percent. Of these, 19 percent were from gated communities. We based our survey questions on the literature on community and on our knowledge of gated communities developed in the first portion of the research process. Our questions concerned motivation, neighborliness, the degree of internal community involvement, the degree of involvement in the outside community, and the perceived effectiveness of the gates.

A Typology of Gated Communities

All walled developments and neighborhoods with security guards do not look alike or serve the same market in the same ways. In our initial reconnaissance of gated areas in early 1994 we found distinct development types serving very different housing markets. All had some system of access control, but they differed substantially in how they addressed the development of a sense of community within their walls.

We found that cities and gated communities can be seen to fall into three main categories. We have labeled them lifestyle communities, prestige communities, and security zone communities. These categories are not based on exclusive and unchanging distinctions. Instead, they are ideal types, designed as aids to understanding rather than as a firm taxonomy. Real developments often exhibit characteristics from more than one type. The three types represent differing physical characteristics and differing motivations of their residents, both of which are closely related to market segments.

Some very large developments are designed to cater to more than one market segment, containing hierarchies of gated areas based on income and lifestyle preferences. Areas that are retrofitted with barricades for an existing rather than an anticipated population sometimes house a mixture of generations and consequently meet multiple housing needs, or they might be changing rapidly, either gentrifying or declining. Inner-city and suburban developments may be retrofitted to meet market or new homeowner demands. Throughout the nation, most of the developments we located were newer subdivisions, purposely designed for a particular clientele; but even those narrowly targeted homogeneous developments vary in their characteristics and have residents with different motivations for living there.

Lifestyle Communities

In lifestyle communities, the gates provide security and separation for the leisure activities and amenities offered within. The lifestyle development is the most common in the Sunbelt but is found throughout the country. There are three distinct types of lifestyle community: the retirement community; the golf and leisure community; and the suburban new town. The first of these, the retirement community, is developed for middle- and upper-middle-class retirees who want structure, recreation, and a built-in social life in their early retirement years. Many of these developments start out as second homes to which their owners eventually retire permanently. As a result, these developments often contain both part-year and year-round residents. Examples are nationwide chains such as Leisure World and Sun City, whose names refer to their intentional retirement character.

The golf and leisure community is exemplified by developments like Blackhawk Country Club near San Francisco, where the golf course and tennis club are central features. Hilton Head and other recreation spots on the South Carolina coast have been noted for their retirement

A lifestyle community: Sun Lakes, Banning, California

and leisure orientations for many years. Even in snowy northern areas, gated country club developments are becoming more common.

The new town is a new class of suburban lifestyle community. It is not the urban village development propagated by the new urbanists like Andres Duany, Peter Calthorpe, and others.[19] The suburban gated new town developments are large, comprising as many as several thousand housing units, and attempt to incorporate both residential and commercial/industrial and retail activities within or adjacent to the development. New towns are not new; but the gating of their residential areas is. One of the earliest and most successful new towns is the Irvine Ranch near Disneyland in Orange County, California. The complex contains both gated and nongated areas. Since the success of Irvine, this form of development has burgeoned throughout the Sunbelt states of California, Arizona, New Mexico, and Texas.

Prestige Communities

Prestige communities are among the fastest-growing development forms in the nation. Their gates symbolize distinction and prestige and create

A prestige community

and protect a secure place on the social ladder. They lack the recreational amenities of the lifestyle communities, often differing little from a standard residential subdivision except for their gates. The gates are motivated by a desire to project an image, protect current investments, and control housing values. They include the enclaves of the rich and famous; developments for the top fifth, the very affluent; and executive home developments for the middle class.

The rich and famous communities are the original gated communities in the United States; they have been with us for decades. They are the small compounds of privacy for celebrities and the gated enclaves of the very rich, and they are found from the hills of Hollywood to the coasts of the Northeast. Highly exclusive, often hidden and heavily defended, they are the model for all the gated communities proliferating across the nation.

The top-fifth and executive communities are meant to confer some of the prestige of the rich and famous enclaves to those with less-exclusive status. The intention is also in part to artificially induce community in an ersatz homogeneous neighborhood, where physical security and social security are enhanced both by sameness and by controlled access. Top-fifth developments are designed for senior executives, managers, and other successful professionals. They feature elaborate gatehouses, monumental entrances, and prestige amenities such as artificial lakes or carefully preserved natural features such as ocean or river fronts and woods. They can be found in most metropolitan areas but are most noticeable around the boom towns of the 1980s like Dallas, Texas.

The executive communities are their wanna-be cousins. Scaled-down versions of top-fifth developments, they are sold by developers as "executive," although they are really just middle-class subdivisions. These are a growing and ever more prominent form of development in many metropolitan areas, including Los Angeles and Orange County, California, and the suburbs of Houston, Dallas, Miami, Chicago, and New York.

Security Zone Communities

In security zone communities the fear of crime and outsiders is the foremost motivation for defensive fortification. This class includes three types: the city perch, the suburban perch, and the barricade perch. We call them perches because it is not the developers who build the gates but the residents, who are often desperately trying to maintain and stay in their neighborhoods. The residents retrofit their neighborhoods with gates or barricades, erecting fortifications to fend off or regain control from some outside threat. By marking their boundaries and restricting access, they attempt to build and strengthen the feeling and function of community in their neighborhood. Security zone gatings and street closures occur at all income levels and in all areas. The disruptions caused by crime and traffic that their residents fear may be real or perceived, near or far; the important point is not whether they *need* to cut off access to their streets, but that they feel they *must*. Major metropolitan areas from Los Angeles to New York have seen the proliferation of this type of development.

In the city, neighborhoods from the most affluent to the most desperately poor are looking to gates as a way to hold off the urban disorder they see around them. Sometimes the threat is on their own doorsteps, sometimes a number of blocks away. Creators of the city perch are looking to protect themselves from crime and from traffic, wanting their homes secure, their streets safe to walk on, their children protected from speeding cars and predators. Sometimes unwilling, sometimes unable

A security-zone community

to flee to the higher ground of the suburbs, they fort up in place. Affluent neighborhoods in Los Angeles and public housing projects in Washington, D.C., among many others, have erected gates.

The suburban perch is a more recent but growing phenomenon, as more and more of the problems previously thought of as urban occur in inner-ring suburbs and smaller towns. In some cases, as the inner suburbs age and urbanize, the quality of life their residents once enjoyed deteriorates. Sometimes residents of older suburban subdivisions fear that they will be next and move to gate their entrances before real trouble reaches their doors. As with the city perches, the danger may be traffic more than crime, as residents fear the impact of overburdened residential streets on their quality of life.

The barricade perch is the fastest-growing type of community in the security zone category. Barricade perches are not fully gated communities; they are not completely walled or fenced and all entrances are not secured with gates. Instead they use barricades to close off some streets. We include them because, like the other forms discussed in this book, barricade perches are intentionally designed security settlements with restricted access to normally public spaces. Partly because of the expense, but often because the neighborhoods exist on public streets, their complete closure is impossible. The barricades create a suburban cul-de-sac pattern out of the city grid and leave just one or two entrances to the neighborhood. The effect is as close to full gating as is practicable. In Miami, Houston, and other cities, dozens of neighborhoods have turned to this solution. In some cities there are long backlogs of neighborhoods waiting for approval of plans to barricade.

Social Values

The three major categories of gated communities—lifestyle, prestige, and security zone—and the nine specific subtypes all reflect to varying degrees four social values (see table 2-2): a sense of community, or the preservation and strengthening of neighborhood bonds; exclusion, or separation and protection from the outside; privatization, or the desire to privatize and internally control public services; and stability, or homogeneity, and predictability. These dimensions relate to the five communal elements described earlier. Where sense of community is a primary value motivating the residents of gated communities, it reflects all five aspects of community: shared territory, shared values, a shared public realm, support structure, and a shared destiny. Exclusion helps define shared territory by separating community members from outsiders. Privatization reflects a desire to protect a shared destiny through increased local control. Stability suggests shared values and support structures, and retaining stability is also a way of protecting shared destiny.

The lifestyle communities attract those who want separate, private services and amenities; they are also seeking a homogeneous, predictable environment. The prestige communities draw those seeking a stable

Table 2-2. *The Importance of Social Values in Residents' Choice of a Gated Community*

Value	Lifestyle	Prestige	Security zone
Sense of Community	Tertiary	Tertiary	Secondary
Exclusion	Secondary	Secondary	Primary
Privatization	Primary	Tertiary	Tertiary
Stability	Secondary	Primary	Secondary

neighborhood of similar people where property values will be protected; concerns about separation and privatization of services come second. The security zone neighborhoods are trying to strengthen and protect a sense of community, but their primary goal is to exclude the places and people they perceive as threats to their safety or quality of life. In the next three chapters, we examine each of the three types in detail.

3

Gates to Paradise
Lifestyle Communities

LIFESTYLE COMMUNITIES are to many the archetypal gated community, the image that first comes to mind. They were the first type of gated community to appear in many areas, and they were the first to spread and proliferate. They emerged from the original Del Webb retirement developments and golf- and leisure-oriented subdivisions in the Sunbelt retirement areas of Florida, the Carolinas, southern California, and Arizona. The developers' primary motivation for designing these settlements was to capitalize on a growing leisure-consuming society. Many are marketed for golfers, retirees, and empty nesters for their "care-free living," "active lifestyle," or members-only golf and country club facilities.

The lifestyle developments are differentiated from the other types of gated communities by their emphasis on amenities. There are three types. The first, the retirement community, is often centered on a golf course and clubhouse, but many include a wide range of recreational amenities and structured programs of social activity. The second type, the golf and leisure community, is similar physically to the retirement development but is marketed to and managed for people of working age, from young families to empty nesters. Golf and leisure communities include gated country clubs, golf developments, and second-home resorts. The third type is the new town. New towns are large master-planned developments that aim to provide residents with a complete living experience, from gated subdivisions to schools, shopping centers, commercial offices, and parks and recreation.

The shared public space in these developments is privatized and controlled, but more as a social statement than as a safety device. The security measures are designed primarily to provide distance from unwanted guests and control of amenities such as lakes or golf courses rather than protection against crime. In fact, few of the upper-end suburban residents in our focus groups had any personal experience with metropolitan turbulence; they had moved to their developments from affluent suburbs and wealthy city districts. They had common lifestyle preferences and carried out this shared destiny through their communal activities.

Catering to a New Leisure Class

Lifestyle communities are part of a broad national socioeconomic transformation. In order to comprehend these specialized developments we must first understand the context from which they spring. Americans are growing richer and poorer. After World War II the American middle class expanded without interruption until the mid-1970s. Fueled by the most productive manufacturing base and the decline of Western Europe's capacity, the United States enjoyed virtual world economic hegemony. Its rapid economic expansion was unparalleled in world history, in particular with respect to the breadth and depth of its effect on the national social order. Americans' incomes rose rapidly, and so did their real wealth. More than 65 percent of Americans owned their own homes through generous government subsidies for home loans. The automobiles, a sign of conspicuous wealth only a decade before the war, became the symbol of middle-class status. And Americans were able to accumulate savings for retirement through hard-fought labor negotiation and the advent of Social Security. The twin economic security factors of rising real wages and the superannuation or retirement benefits through public and private employment empowered the middle class to use its disposable income in ways unthinkable in previous eras. America's working class adults could relieve their children of the burden of supporting them in their old age; they could choose where to live; they could retire with dignity anywhere.

Although gains in household income slowed after 1973 and have gone disproportionately to those in upper income brackets, the changes in standard of living have still been great. Between 1973 and 1993 the average individual after-tax income, in constant dollars, has nearly doubled.[1] Although these changes are now taken for granted, their effects have been profound. Not only has disposable income risen dramatically; so have the conditions associated with having more money: we live longer, consume more, and live healthier lives. The American middle class has become to some extent a leisure class, able to engage in leisure activities beyond the scope of any people in the world. Housing developers have been able to mass-produce housing based on a leisure-time model, incorporating garages, work rooms, and game and television rooms into ordinary dwellings. Special automobiles are designed for leisure driving, such as station wagons, vans, and trucks to pull boats.

The explosion in leisure living was soon incorporated into housing developments in the suburbs, where developers attempted to create woodsy open spaces with artificial lakes, planted forests, and man-made streams. Leisure lifestyles created a demand for second-home housing developments away from the primary domicile. This movement spawned two kinds of new patterns—the snow birds and the ski water bunnies. Snow birds were first sighted in the recreation areas of California and Florida, where older midwesterners and easterners migrated during the harsh northern winters. The ski water bunnies were so named for their weekend snow skiing in winter and water skiing in summer. Their second homes, used for vacations during middle age, often became their permanent homes after retirement. Housing designed for part-year use was being converted to year-round occupancy.

Developers were quick to see the potential in these changes. Increasingly, in response to the rising affluence of the middle class, second-home and even retirement-home developments sprang up all over the South, Southwest, and West Coast. These developments were differentiated by market segment. Some were designed to appeal exclusively to the growing number of younger retirees with part- or full-year occupancy potential. Another class of development was fashioned for the sports-minded, middle-class, white-collar work force that could afford to live near recreation—golf, boating, or fishing. Lifestyle, not mere shelter, became a major feature of development.

The rise of the upper middle class has continued even while the working middle class shrinks. The scale of this transformation is difficult to fathom. It has already established its presence on the American landscape in the form of the housing and settlement types it creates. Entire cities and subregions are devoted to catering to new retirees and new millionaires. These developments are intentionally homogeneous to reflect the choices of the occupiers for people and place. The gate is an adjunct to this new class-conscious development.

Retirement Communities

Retirement communities, from the nationwide chain of Leisure Worlds to individual developments, have been the prototype for exclusionary living for the middle class. There were 33 million people age sixty-five and older in 1994, or one of every eight Americans. Most of these seniors live independently. The average retirement age has dropped, and life expectancy has risen. Americans who reach sixty-five years of age can now expect to live seventeen more years. And incomes have also risen: from 1957 to 1992 income in constant 1992 dollars more than doubled, from $6,537 to $14,548 for men and $3,409 to $8,189 for women. While disparities exist among the elderly based on race, ethnicity, marital status, work history, and other factors, all groups showed improvement in economic status during the 1980s.[2] Retirees are living longer and better than ever before. Retirees are a class with preferences and the ability to make choices. They have their own periodicals and organizations, such as the American Association of Retired Persons (AARP), that wield enormous political and social clout. They live all over the country and sometimes have more than one domicile. However, they prefer warm areas with low taxes and high security. Many retirees reside in the warmer climates of California, Arizona, Nevada, Texas, and Florida. States and many cities are advertising for retirees because they bring such an economic boon. Age restrictions,

A lifestyle community

security patrols, and gates and walls create nearly self-sufficient enclaves of senior housing.

At Leisure World in Silver Spring, Maryland, security guards board the public buses that serve the development, making sure that no "undesirables" use the buses to enter. The borders are marked by gates, walls, fences, ditches, and barricades. Retirement developments like Leisure World have thousands of residents living in housing designed for a range of incomes and lifestyles, with dozens of social clubs and recreational activities. They are the residential equivalent of a cruise vacation: a standardized product, offering an all-inclusive package with no surprises. According to one resident, "I like the organized type of lifestyle. It's well structured and managed. When you get to be my age, you've had all the freewheeling you can stand."[3]

Skidaway Island, off the Georgia coast, has several developments designed for the upmarket retiree. The Landings on Skidaway Island is a gated golf preserve marketed to active, affluent seniors through advertisements in the *New York Times Magazine*. Like many upscale retirement developments, it has a high proportion of second-home buyers. The Landings ads, like most, speak of leisure activity rather than security. The retirement developments that do broach the security issue do it obliquely, as in an ad for Crystal Tree, a suburban Chicago retirement development: "From the moment you drive up to gatehouse and are greeted by the friendly security guard, you sense it. The feeling that here all is safe, free from worry."[4]

This Is Easy Street: Mission Hills Country Club, Rancho Mirage, California

Mission Hills Country Club is a sprawling development next to a lush golf course; the vista from nearly any of the narrow internal roads is of greens and palm trees. Rancho Mirage is one of the wealthier of the small contiguous towns of California's Coachella Valley, just a mile or two from Palm Springs.

There are three gates into the walled development, each with a staffed guardhouse. The main entrance road turns past several fairways and through areas of prosperous but not showy homes. It leads to the Mission Hills Country Club, itself a showy desert stucco building fronted with tall columns and even taller palm trees. The lobby is decorated in the tasteful, luxurious, but unremarkable style of upper-middle-class hotel chains.

We met with some residents in the Dinah Shore Room; with its long wooden table and castered armchairs, it had the feeling of an executive board room. This feeling was heightened by the residents themselves, who were all white, male, and in their sixties and seventies. They looked fit and tanned in their golf and tennis shirts and their pressed knee-length shorts. All were or had been active on the homeowner association boards in their various areas, which they called "phases," using the developer's terminology. There is no central homeowner association in MHCC, but rather fifteen independent boards governing individual areas. Despite this lack of centralization, and despite the large size of MHCC, most of the men were acquainted with each other. They were a pleasant and thoughtful group, discussing their health problems and golf games with each other when we arrived.

Almost all reported that security was the primary reason they moved into Mission Hills. As retirees, they worried about crime, especially when away on vacation or at their primary homes elsewhere. They like the maintenance-free lifestyle, the aesthetics of the development, and the amenities, especially the golf club. Everyone agrees that the recreational amenities are key. The reputation of the place was a consideration for these men as well. One says, "I found that prestige-wise, when we go places and can say we live in the Mission Hills Country Club, it's an added benefit."

Only one man says that security was a minor consideration. "This was the last place in the world I ever thought I'd live. I never conceived of living in a gated community. It went counter to all my social and political philosophies." But now, he says, "I like the mode of life. I think it's conducive to good health and longevity." He finds he gets more exercise since he moved to Mission Hills. "You can't avoid it. It's not a compelling need, you have nothing else to do."

When questioned about any disadvantages of living in their desert resort, the group falls uncharacteristically silent. Hesitantly, someone mentions that the CC&Rs mean that you give up a certain amount of privacy and control. The rest second this, but the discussion quickly turns to what is good about the CC&Rs, and then to what is good about Mission Hills. They talk more about the recreation and the nearness of quality medical facilities.

Participation: The Outlook at MHCC

The residents of MHCC are still active in every sense of the word. They were active in their previous community and business lives, and they bring that same energy to their new home. Several take exception to the concern that MHCC residents are withdrawing. "We're interested in the outside community," exclaims one of the younger men, to enthusiastic nods from the group. "I think we're all aware of what's happening in the Coachella Valley. And I think we also take advantage of the many facilities here in the valley in terms of dining places, entertainment facilities, things like that." There is a chorus of agreement.

Asked about city politics, one man argues, "I think our residents here are more involved and concerned about the city of Rancho Mirage and who our representatives are and how they are doing things than anyone else on the outside. I don't think we're isolating ourselves from the community." Another notes that they have the same sheriff, the same fire department, the same everything as the people who live across the street from their gates. As for their relationship with the county, well, "You pay your taxes."

Their connection extends beyond politics, says one man. "My guess is we're more proactive than any of your other garden-variety communities. We're all retired, we have time. But I think also the group of people out here, most of them are accomplished professionals of one type or another—people who whatever they did in life they did it well. They have a lot of energy left, and they're still interested in doing stuff." He volunteers locally as a literacy tutor. Although none of the other men at the table has such involvements, he says he knows of many in the development who do.

Self-Government: The Inlook at MHCC

Most of their energy seems to go into the management and governance of Mission Hills itself. This is a special group, among the most active in their development, all with long commitments to their various associations. This is no light task, they want to tell us. "If you have any sense of responsibility, you must devote hundreds of hours, and I mean hundreds of hours, to various committees and boards."

Participation in general varies widely. "In every association, there's one or two people who do spend a great deal of time attending the meetings whether they're on the board or not. You have your town criers and your people who want to get involved in every issue, and then you have the people who do live here for retirement, and believe me, being on the board is a thankless job." As in so many homeowner associations, the problem of a volunteer self-government is sustaining resident interest and involvement. "Continuity is a problem, because a lot of people here are retired, and they don't want to be committed to longer than two years at a time to homeowners' meetings and gate committee meetings and this meeting and that meeting because it does interfere partially with their retirement."

The group is eager to talk about the issues they face as board and committee members. Most involve the divisions among the different homeowner associations, unmediated by any umbrella association. A byzantine dues structure, which is based on the age of the phase and the services included, causes resentments and competition. "It can be difficult, and, depending on who you talk to, pretty inequitable in terms of how the infrastructure is cared for." The older phases "don't choose to participate in some of the infrastructure things." For instance, one new phase pays entirely for a gate near the country club, despite the fact that it is halfway across the development, solely because the gate was built at a time when the cost could be attached to the new phase then being built.

Primarily there are the difficulties getting the associations to work together. One security firm patrols the entire development, but all other services, from property management to landscaping, are provided separately. "If you want to do something that has something to do with everyone, you have to get fifteen associations to agree to it." They spent two years just working out a cable deal. Small coalitions of three or four associations that border each other do occasionally form, such as when adjoining phases contract with the same company to trim trees. "But people here tend to be autonomous in the associations. They're composed of successful people who've been in business, and they like to think they know how to run their little ship, and they don't care how this other guy runs his ship."

A few years ago the associations formed a gate committee, the only governing entity that serves the entire development. It is purely ad hoc, however, made up of representatives of the interested association boards. The committee goes over financial statements and reviews issues and problems with the security firm. They meet irregularly, from every two weeks during the winter months to not at all during the summer.

The gate committee is not the only thing that goes into hibernation for the summer. The high proportion of part-time second-home owners means that many concerns, and even some services, are put on hold during the summer months. The year-round retirees resent the seasonal involvement of the part-timers, who seem to have less of a vested interest in keeping the place up. A resident complains that they are likely to say, "'The heck with the flowers in the summertime,' because they're not here in the summer."

Rancho Mirage has a median income of $42,000, putting it in the top 15 percent of cities by income in the nation, but still there are sometimes residents for whom the Mission Hills lifestyle is an expense that they can only barely afford. For some, this is a group that creates problems, but in at least one association, neighborly concern is the answer. "When we go to pass an assessment, we always take into consideration the group within our phase who perhaps could not meet that casually, so we try to make adjustment so that it will work for everybody. It's a serious thing to consider."

The divisions between the full- and part-timers and among the associations do not extend into the social life of Mission Hills. "Obviously you get to know your neighbors, but I don't think you're bound by your homeowner association. We're all so close to each other," explains one man. To one of the residents, Mission Hills is a small world. "After you live here a few years, in my opinion, it begins to be like a Peyton Place. . . . Socially you get to know what everyone is doing." The rest of the group laughs at the analogy, and he quickly adds, "I'm not being critical when I say that." Another agrees. "It's like a town within a town."

Others say that community and neighborliness revolve around lifestyle choices. "I think it has to do with your recreational interests. People who play golf tend to congregate, people who play tennis tend to congregate."

In the end, these men did not come to Mission Hills to find a small-town community. They came for manicured greens, the built-in social life, the many amenities. It is the list of the affluent retiree: "The gate, the golf, the tennis, the ability to drive around in a golf cart . . . there's many days when I never move my regular car. It's a different lifestyle, and I bought the lifestyle."

Golf and Leisure Communities

Although many retirement developments include a golf course and recreational facilities, they are distinguished by their focus on a social environment designed for seniors. Other suburban developments are aimed at a younger market with the disposable income and interest to support golf courses and other recreational amenities. Many are resort developments, providing second homes in vacation settings to the growing number of Americans able to afford it.

Taking their cue from the gated compounds of the elite and the patrolled retirement developments, more and more of these leisure-oriented developments are gated, reflecting a notion of shared territory and exclusive rather than inclusive sharing of values. These are the golf and leisure communities, spawned by the upscale real estate boom of the

Entrance to a golf leisure community at Dove Canyon, Orange County, California

1980s. First built in the Sunbelt, gated golf communities have become common around Chicago and other northern cities and are being developed in Iowa and Minnesota. Gates provide status and prestige, creating large, imposing, ornamented entryways to the country club lifestyle.

Living in an exclusive development or owning a vacation home is now part of the affluent lifestyle. In 1992 almost 35 percent of all middle-class Americans considered having a vacation home to be an essential lifestyle feature, up 10 percent over the previous decade.[5] Although developers are finding it hard to build affordable homes for the average American, there is no dearth of market for resort properties. One reason for this is that upper-middle-class Americans have so much disposable income—nearly $2,000–$8,000 per month.

As a result, moderately wealthy people in their early forties are able to afford high-status properties that they live in for only part of the year. Some of the more specialized golf and leisure communities are resort developments, designed for second-home buyers. With extensive amenities for leisure activities, they are usually located in the Sunbelt and offer security designed to protect property during long periods without anyone in residence. The developments on Hilton Head Island, South Carolina, are of this type, as are developments in the Rancho Mirage and Palm Springs area of California. Another type is the sports enclave, such as the Polo Grounds in Boca Raton, Florida. These developments have championship-quality courses and fields with tournament facilities and pride themselves on being host to national competitions. They tend to be at the upper end of the price range and boast elaborate architecture, gatehouses, and security systems.

"Members only" moves to another dimension when the greens, the club, and the streets are all access-controlled. Many of these developments also offer tennis clubs, swimming complexes, and other recreational facilities. Some who buy into these developments are golfers, but many others simply value the open space and greenery golf courses provide. The often luxurious clubhouses are a particular draw: "It goes back to when we were kids and all wanted to belong to a special club— a place where you feel special and not everybody can come into. That's the basis you start with, and it works whether you are talking about a club like this or about your favorite neighborhood bar."[6]

The prestige and sense of belonging that come from living in a country club development are important factors in their appeal, and partially explain why such a high proportion is gated. Even in large developments where only a minority of residents actually golf, the club atmosphere starts at the gate and extends through the development. Blackhawk Country Club is an example of such a development.

The Clubhouse: Blackhawk Country Club, San Ramon, California

Blackhawk is a sprawling, golf-centered development of more than 4,000 acres nestled in the hills near Mt. Diablo, almost an hour east of downtown San Francisco. Blackhawk was designed to tap the growing market of wealthy venture capitalists and inventors of Silicon Valley and San Francisco. The developer, Ken Bering, reasoned that this new class of executive needed a new housing pattern that took advantage of the natural surroundings and offered additional private amenities.

The result is a manicured and sanitized high-income environment with clubhouse, golf course, and tennis club. A short distance from the gates sits Blackhawk Center, with upscale shopping, restaurants, a cineplex, commercial office space, and an antique car museum. Houses in its subdivisions range in price from $300,000 to more than $5 million. The bottom end of this price scale is not unusual in a county where the average income is $55,000, but most of the houses sell for far more. In addition to the main gated entrance staffed with a guard, three of the higher-priced subdivisions have their own guarded gates, and several others have unmanned electronic gates.

Blackhawk has been written about by real estate magazines and discussed in Joel Garreau's *Edge City*.[7] It is home to professional athletes, entertainers, computer millionaires, and ordinary upper-middle-class executives and professionals. Outsiders as well as its residents consider it a place for the nouveau riche. To the residents, this means they are less snobby and elitist than the old money, country club set. Blackhawk's carefully crafted image may be that of an exclusive, private country club, but only about a third of the residents actually golf. Those who do would rather be ten minutes from a golf course than an hour closer to work. The others buy in for the lifestyle of sports and club activities, the prestige, and the location far from city crowds but near cultural and recreational destinations.

We met some representatives of Blackhawk's lifestyle at the home of one of our key informants. She and her husband have lived in the development for more than five years and know it well. The small group gathered in the living room in a shirt-sleeve session in the early fall. The house was not large but was well appointed, fitting their empty-nester status. There was a small pool off the family room but no views of the nearby golf course. The group of couples filtered in slightly late, all dressed in standard after-work casuals.

Despite the way gates seem to dominate everything about Blackhawk, fear and security are not defining characteristics and were not central reasons any of these residents chose Blackhawk. They chose it for the country club setting, the golf, the tennis, the look and feel of the place, and its reputation. As Al, a well-groomed and tanned golfer, explained, the gate "has nothing in my mind to do with the home I live in. . . . I like the ambiance and the persona that this development has. It's my personal choice." His wife, Susie, agreed. "I think we'd like it equally well even if the gate wasn't there. . . . The gate is kind of incidental. Perhaps we would vote that it was better, but I think that it wouldn't have been a determining factor, we wouldn't have said we won't move in if it didn't have the gate."

For George and Laura, the strong CC&Rs were the key selling point. They lived for many years in an nongated subdivision in a nearby suburb and were bothered by neighbors who were lax in grooming their yards as well as the amount of traffic on the streets. Then a proposal to use an existing house as a senior care home got the neighborhood up in arms. They failed to block it, and that was the last straw. "It was a lack of control is what it was. You could not maintain the environment you thought you had moved into."

Appreciation for the gates and the security they represent came later. All agreed with one woman that "security is becoming increasingly more important in recent years, which it wasn't when the development was originally built." One man, the owner of a contracting firm, is clear what his vote would be. "I don't think I'd get rid of it. I like the idea of limited access." He moved here for the lifestyle and tight CC&Rs but found that after moving in the security "really started to matter." According to George, security in Blackhawk "comes from knowing that if you see someone on the street, you know they're OK." Laura says the only thing she worries about is mountain lions. "Contrast that with San Francisco. I wouldn't talk to anyone on the street there during the day."

Community at the Clubhouse

Similar to other large golf developments we visited, interaction seems to center on recreation: the clubhouse, the golf course, and the tennis courts. For some, this makes a community. "You live with the people you play with, so you do have that sense of community," explained one woman. "We've become friends with people from all over the community because we are in Blackhawk, and I don't know if we would have met as many people and become friends with as many people [if we lived elsewhere]."

Another woman agrees that there is a neighborly feeling in Blackhawk, but her husband takes exception. "I don't know," he says, "if we have many real friends here." A moment of embarrassed silence falls. The couple quickly explain that they are very busy and usually go away on the weekends.

The limited access ensures that all inside are preapproved, and the leisure amenities provide a ground for meeting at least a subset of one's neighbors. And if living behind two gates is not enough, it is easy to withdraw even further. One man, who refused to tell us what city he worked in or even his profession, clearly wants minimal contact. As he said, "It's a really independent group here, and it's a setting where you can get into your own thing, and you don't have to be really a participant in any community activity, even inside Blackhawk."

Blackhawk is not just a group of neighbors. It is the organizational equivalent of a small town, with its own homeowner association and board of directors, its own rules and police force, and its own infrastructure to maintain. But within Blackhawk, the tight restrictions, master planning, and high incomes mean that the messy politics of the average town can be avoided. Association meetings are not well attended, and most residents ignore internal politics. To these residents, this lack of involvement signals a well-managed environment. Perhaps an affluent gated community like Blackhawk doesn't need as much community steering as others might, volunteers Jim, the contractor. Residents feel little need to get involved. The security company, the property management company, and the maintenance companies have all been hired to take care of matters so the residents don't have to.

If people's connections within Blackhawk seem tenuous, the connections to the adjacent city of Danville and the rest of the outside world are even more so. "I feel part of Blackhawk. I don't feel part of Danville as a whole," said one resident. Those with children have to be more involved, they all agree, but they themselves are not, and they offer no apologies for this. They deeply resent local politicians and local government. When one man refers to a strikingly designed and even more strikingly expensive new city hall in the next town, he sets off a round of passionate complaints about egos and waste.

They do not say that they are loath to vote for a tax or bond issue that will benefit the county of which they are part, but all are quick to defend their right not to. "It's your prerogative," says one man. Whatever the reason for a bond or tax hike, he thinks, chances are that the private virtual town of Blackhawk already provides equivalent service within its boundaries. "The gate gives you an option, and you don't have to feel guilty about it either way."

These are angry voters, cynical about politics and tired of paying into the community chest. "People are tired of the way the government has managed the issues and the freedom the voters have given them to do things. Because it's been so mismanaged, and because you don't really have control over how the money is spent. I feel disenfranchised. If the courts are going to release criminals, and we're going to continue not to prosecute people, and continue spending money the way we're spending it, and I can't impact it, and I've worked on campaigns, if I can't have any control, therefore I'm going to put myself in a situation where I feel I have a little more control over how I live my life."

A woman who works for the federal government expresses similar resentment: "I'm sick of giving, just sick of giving. There's a point you have to stop, start thinking of ourselves, our retirement. I used to be more likely to vote for things for other people."

Later in our conversation, her husband defends her stance. "You withdraw from the bigger picture and being involved, and maybe being elbow to elbow with maybe a bad setting economically or whatever it happens to be. But the same time, if you are a voting individual, you're involved in the state setting and the initiatives and referendums, you are paying your taxes, maybe support Three Strikes and You're Out [the initiative passed in California to incarcerate third-time felons for life], maybe you're active in the campaign against immigration. Do you have to be involved in the nitty gritty and see it every day? If you're aware of it, and still involved in the state or local government through elections or if you're active in campaigns, aren't you doing the same thing?"

This group, while repeatedly emphasizing how pleasant it is to be in Blackhawk, isolated from the unpleasantness of the metropolitan region outside, is nevertheless determined to convince us that they are not disconnected, that they have not withdrawn. One says, "You are going out on a daily basis to the world at large, so you're not insulating yourself and having your whole life revolve around what's inside the gate. You can't ignore it, and you don't ignore it." But at another point in the evening, she describes her reaction to working in the outside world: "I don't like going to San Francisco. I don't feel comfortable in San Francisco. I don't leave my building when I get there, except to come home." Her husband does venture out of his building at lunch time; but he says, "It's almost a release and relief to come back here. You're dealing with elements that are sometimes very undesirable. It's like the old moat and castle. You get back to your spot and you feel secure."

Our hostess tells us that there are many people in Blackhawk who do just stay inside, who leave as little as possible. When they do venture out, it is usually to the commercial center just outside the gates. She says that she would never have moved to Blackhawk when she had small children at home, because she wouldn't have wanted that much of a homogeneous environment. But, she says, there are a lot of people who do.

Control

The key to Blackhawk is control. The gate, the guards, and the rules all create an environment where there are no surprises. The attraction is the "lack of chaos; it brings in structure." This is something all agree on. "It's nice at least part of the day to be able to come into something where you know what to expect, that you can count on it, and that is calming."

To one man, the uniformity and strict control of upkeep and outside appearance is a comfort he values highly. "I don't think it's so much the gated community, it's the desire for the discipline, the work ethic, whatever you want to call it, for having that consistency throughout the community. It makes you feel you're with people that have a common bond with you, regardless of race or ethnicity." His wife is more ambivalent, pointing out that the tight controls also attract the sort of person who is fairly rigid as to what he or she will tolerate. For instance, there have been problems over their dog barking, and some of their neighbors have been "vicious."

The group tells as many stories about being glad for the rules as being inconvenienced by them, but the benefits outweigh the problems, they all assert.

The controls extend beyond property appearance to personal behavior. Trash cans may be put out only during certain hours; no campers, commercial vehicles, or on-street parking is allowed; and door-to-door canvassing is strictly banned. There have been food drives for the poor, but those have been conducted at the main entrance. Even Blackhawk Girl Scouts must sell their wares from the other side of the gates, hawking their cookies to the cars waiting to enter. It's a privacy issue, says one resident. "Everyone has a right to have their own independence and choose who and when they want to interact with. No one has a right to impose on you a setting that you don't want to experience." The world inside the gates is sacrosanct.

Small Town Nostalgia

A resident who recently visited West Virginia recounts how impressed he was by the community spirit in the small towns there. He thinks Blackhawk is similar. "It's an artificial setting here, but you're creating that environment, which duplicates what Middle America used to be back when you had small towns." The rest of the group eagerly picks up on the small-town analogy.

One reminisces about growing up in rural Monterey County, where they never locked their doors, knew everyone, and felt a sense of real community. Another recalled the Blackhawk area twenty-five years earlier, before the suburban sprawl transformed it, when it had a more small-town feeling. Blackhawk, with its gates and master plan, seems to them a way to hold on to that feeling. Its growth limits are set, its club memberships limited, so they will never feel crowded or surrounded by too many strangers.

The image of Blackhawk as small town is part of the residents' shared values. They know what to expect and where they can have an impact if they want to. A resident explains that she had never attended city council meetings in the suburb where she previously lived but now regularly attends homeowner association meetings. "Maybe because it is a little more manageable, and it isn't a nebulous thing out there, you can put your hands on it."

To an outsider, Blackhawk may seem more like an exclusive club than a small town, but to its residents, it's the closest thing to community they think they may ever find in today's world.

Gated New Towns: Commodified Community

Large-scale master-planned developments have always attempted to provide a community or town flavor. Master-planned developments are increasingly presenting the home buyer with "a complete package." Housing developers are faced with the need to sell more than the shelter. They market not just homes in a carefully planned environment, but a total living experience. This is the new town as lifestyle. As reflected in advertising and the complexity of design and amenities, the commodity they are selling is not just houses, but a community.

This style of large-scale building is now the major force in the housing marketplace. The Newhall Land and Farming Company and the Irvine Company, both of southern California, were the first to see this and build total citylike developments. Large-scale public companies like Home Federal Savings and Loan are investing some of their considerable resources into building complete towns that include schools, parks, and similar amenities. In Orange County, California, the major developers are building entire cities, with populations of up to 40,000. Disney is building its own city, called Celebration, near Orlando, Florida. In the mid-1990s, hundreds of such projects were under construction across the country. As the home has been commodified, so has the nature of community.

A gate and wall or other control point is a part of many of these developments and part of the marketing package. More recent new towns have "villages" as gated subdivisions, offering exclusionary status to the most expensive housing. These tracts are of three types: "urban" villages of high-density townhouses that are sometimes gated; "luxury" villages, oriented around golf or perhaps a lake, almost always gated; and "resort" villages, designed as second-home developments, with high-end amenities, including gatehouses.[8] In California and Arizona, where gated communities are common, the new towns include gates on middle-price tracts as well.

Redwood Shores in Redwood City, California, is a planned community of apartments, townhouses, and single-family homes on the wetlands of San Francisco Bay. Wide divided streets pass by mirrored midrise office towers and on to the residential developments built around streams and canals. Two of Redwood Shores' subdivisions are gated. One, Lakeshore Villas, is a mid-priced development. The other, Shorebird Island, is a luxury type, completely surrounded by water, its single family homes accessible only by a private gated bridge.

Green Valley, outside Las Vegas, Nevada, is a master-planned development that will have 60,000 residents by the year 2005. Walls are everywhere in Green Valley, with elaborate specifications in the master plan for their composition, height, and design. The CC&Rs prohibit homeowners from changing them in any way, including banning any openings in backyard walls. A marketing agent explains the appeal: "It's safe here. And clean. And nice. The schools are good and the crime rate is low. It's what buyers are looking for."[9]

The high-end tracts of Green Valley have gates as well as walls. A ten-year-old resident complains that his friends cannot get in to see him unless a call is made to the "policeman in the guardhouse." But the walls and gates of Green Valley cannot keep it completely safe; in recent years the community has dealt with a serial rapist, robberies, domestic murder, drugs in the schools, and a toxic cloud of chlorine gas released from a nearby chemical plant.[10]

Silver Creek Valley Country Club, in San Jose, California, epitomizes the self-contained new town. Planned for more than 1,500 units, it includes a host of amenities behind a twenty-four-hour gatehouse. Eventually, it will have a public elementary school and some commercial development on site, with separate entrances for those who live outside the development. Its marketing never mentions gates or security but emphasizes leisure amenities. Equity memberships in its golf course, tennis club, and country club are available only to residents. Tracts range from $300,000 townhouses to $500,000–$700,000 estate homes to custom homesites where the final cost is expected to top $1 million. Two of the subdivisions have their own interior gates, and perimeter fences surround individual tracts as well as the entire development. Security was tight from the beginning, when only a few dozen homes were occupied—home shoppers had to register at the information pavilion outside and carry a pass at all times while inside the gates.[11]

A Down-to-Earth "Paradise": Canyon Lake, California

Canyon Lake, a new town in southern California, is not one of the newest, but it is an excellent example of the type. The developer has incorporated many of the amenities of a city, including a shopping center and a commercial office development. Like other new towns, it includes a range of housing types, differentiated by size, style, and especially income level. Canyon Lake is also the oldest example of a growing trend in large suburban development: its residential area is entirely enclosed behind fences and gates.

Canyon Lake is a gated community of more than 10,000 residents that is also an incorporated town. It bills itself as a "Bit of Paradise," but it is not the upscale development that one might expect in a gated city. Although Canyon Lake includes upscale elements, it has always had a

New town: Canyon Lake, California
Scott Robinson/NYT Pictures

range of socioeconomic groups. Its residents are firemen and police officers, school teachers, engineers, salespersons, retirees, carpenters, technicians, and realtors.

They live in a beautiful setting around a man-made reservoir with a fifteen-mile shoreline, about sixty miles east of Orange County in the desert of southern California. Canyon Lake was created almost twenty-five years ago by a private developer as a secure recreation development for moderate-income urbanites fleeing Los Angeles. The gates were installed to attract part-time residents. In fact, originally, the development was only partially fenced. As permanent residential settlement increased, so did the demand for better fencing and security to separate the development from the troubled low-income cities of Elsinore and Perris nearby. By 1990, Canyon Lake was almost completely built out, and its residents were growing frustrated with and fearful of the local governments. Believing they lived in a private community and should have total control over their destiny, they resented the county government's occasional intrusions into zoning matters, and they feared that Elsinore or Perris might attempt to annex Canyon Lake. Their response was to incorporate.

Canyon Lake became a full-fledged city in 1991. The new city had almost no tax base, but it did not need one. The property owners' association (POA) remains the de facto government, with a budget of $7 million from dues; in comparison, the city generates only $1 million from taxes. The city government is responsible for intergovernmental relations, the small amount of incorporated land that lies outside the POA's fenced domain, and the small police force that is hired under contract from Elsinore. The POA does everything else: maintaining the streets, parks, and landscaping; setting speed limits and issuing fines; overseeing the private security patrol; enforcing the CC&Rs; and operating the golf course and several small businesses. Inside the fence, as the City Manager Jeff Bureau puts it, "the POA runs the show."

City Problems in a Gated City

Jon Gee was the mayor of Canyon Lake when we visited. He is a young man of easy charm who exudes a certain intensity. He is committed to the community life in a very clear-eyed manner. He is no civic booster but sees in Canyon Lake a kind of middle-class preserve, a "Leave It to Beaver" lifestyle that may be an artifact of a previous era. He wants to keep it that way. He likes the land and the people; the town, he believes, is a perfect place to raise his two children.

However, Canyon Lake is maturing, and Mayor Gee knows it has the same problems as any aging suburban area—rising crime, youth delinquency, increasing demands for senior-citizen and other social services. The city has had four murders over the years and has about the same burglary rate as any middle-class suburb in Orange or Riverside County. Graffiti is a growing problem. The fence around the development is easily penetrable. Because of the size of Canyon Lake, such a large volume of traffic passes through its three gates that guards are less than thorough in screening entrants. Access by unauthorized drivers is not entirely thwarted.

The executive director of the POA, Marty Hall, notes that the gates are increasingly important to Canyon Lake residents—perhaps too important. "The gates give people a false sense of security. Some of our residents tell me that they relax as soon as they get beyond the gate." He worries about this because "there is no 100 percent security." He points out the murders and other crimes in the area, acknowledging that the town of 10,000 people has all of the same problems that places outside the gate have. "We have drugs and other issues to deal with here too. The gates don't keep out the world outside."

The reality of these problems was made clear at a meeting of the Canyon Lake Disaster Coordinating Committee. One of the volunteer coordinators, an energetic senior citizen, offered two preparedness reports. Her first report was on disaster and emergency supplies. After a brief discussion of inventory and costs, she reported the theft of the emergency equipment and the food supplies she had just described. Thieves had switched the locks on the storage shed and then stolen a generator, bedding, and other materials while volunteers were trying to find who had replaced the locks. "This was obviously an inside job," she observed. "We have asked all of our community volunteers to keep their eyes open with respect to this equipment. We know some kids have this stuff and we have asked parents to report anything new around the house or garage." This ended the first report.

She opened her next report, on firstaid and volunteer training. After another brief discussion of the operations of the volunteers and their training, she matter-of-factly informed the meeting: "We cannot continue our volunteer training for now. Someone took the video player out of this building. We use the videos for our training programs. It was stolen from the closet." She pointed to a door behind her. "The first-aid classes are also canceled."

One would have thought that two reports of theft would create some discussion and even dismay in a gated, security-guarded community. However, the reports were taken in stride. The city manager raised his eyebrows. The police captain shook his head. But no one raised any questions or seemed surprised by either report. Behind gates with cruising security guards, heavy equipment was being pilfered from civic facilities without much reaction.

The Children behind the Gate

A group of junior-high-school students at a bus stop offered their own insights into the good and the bad of their town. Noisy, vivacious, wearing jeans and backpacks, they looked like kids in any suburb anywhere. They had no fear or wariness of us as strangers. They were curious and eager to talk, which they did all at once. The fence around the town, they all agreed, was not much of a barrier. As one tall girl said, "It's full of holes. Anyone can get through it." A small young boy bragged, "I go in and out of it all of the time."

"The fence isn't as tough as these new Wells Fargo cops," a dark-haired girl said, referring to the POA's private security patrol. She went on to add that the Wells Fargo cops were a lot tougher—unnecessarily tougher—than the old Pinkerton cops. All of the kids agreed they didn't like the new cops. Nevertheless, the fence, if less intimidating than the security patrol, at least kept out some "creeps."

Almost all liked the gate. In their view it was a necessity, a means of keeping the streets safe inside the development. "We don't want the same thing here as outside," said one girl. Outside was Elsinore, which they perceived as a "gang place" where the streets were not safe. When asked if bad things ever happened inside the fence, the kids were perplexed at first. Then they said, "of course." "We even had murders in here," one of the boys volunteered. The kids report that although there are no gangs in Canyon Lake, there is still a curfew, because "some kids get into bad stuff."

A few thought the fence and gates were a nuisance, but most of their complaints echoed those of suburban kids everywhere: nothing to do, nowhere to hang out, "awful" cliques. They wanted a mall to go to, but they were not sure that they would change anything else. They were safe in Canyon Lake, and the rest of the world, viewed with skepticism and a bit of fear, was outside.

Community, Not Neighborhood

In Mayor Gee's view, Canyon Lake is a community but not a neighborhood. He reasons, "The design of the place is so suburban that neighborliness is discouraged. You meet people through events and not by over-the-fence backyard conversations." It is a typical low-density suburb, without sidewalks. The wide curving streets mean that movement within the city, even to visit a close neighbor, is easier by car than by foot. Despite this, both the mayor and the city manager, Jeff Butzlaff, find the community spirit remarkable.

Jeff Butzlaff claims that people within the compound bond readily, irrespective of background. There are more than fifty clubs and associations, and community spirit is generated through organizations and associations rather than neighborliness. The reason for this, he suggests, is that many of the residents are part of two-income households and drive as much as 100 miles in each direction to work in Los Angeles and Orange Counties or even San Diego; they only have time to interact on weekends or in selected groups. Despite this, Jeff remarks, "They are involved people. If you need a committee, we get plenty of active, usually retiree, volunteers." Some of this comes from the large, relatively affluent middle-class retirement base of Canyon Lake. And volunteerism was one of the historic bases of the city. Volunteers helped develop the golf course and provided the labor for most of the city street landscaping and shrubbery. Civic involvement is expected of residents, and because the burden is widely shared, people are generally willing to participate. However, as the housing stock turns over, the more recent and usually more affluent residents do not share the same sense of civic involvement. Jeff admits on a ride around the development that some of the newcomers are here "only because of the fence."

To Marty Hall, the executive director of the POA, the social organization of the development is the most critical element. "The physical side of things is in place," he says. He sees his major task as trying to imbue more residents with community spirit. The city manager and he agree that Canyon Lake is a tight and friendly community, with a strong sense of volunteerism; but as is true everywhere, some people are always involved and some never are.

Canyon Lakers are also more engaged with the surrounding area than their fence and gate might indicate. They shop and eat in Elsinore, share a school district with it, and are active in local political life. Many of Canyon Lake's pioneers established themselves in the local political scene well before cityhood and remain tied to the fabric of the larger community. The interaction between Canyon Lake citizens and residents of nearby localities is largely amicable. The conflicts tend to be over such things as the use of jet skis on the upper reservoir and litter and loud music on the shores of an area adjoining the city boundary. The problems also tend to be youth-related, like most of the problems within the gates. Marty's other major concern is developing more recreational activities and other outlets for kids and teenagers.

The gates cannot keep out all problems, and they do nothing to solve those that arise inside the fence. Most residents put their faith into the physical boundary, the systems to control access. But Marty Hall knows that the real job is to develop social responsibility and community structure. No fence will ever be high enough and no gate strong enough.

Community behind the Lifestyle Gates

Gates add a level of satisfaction to the lifestyle social environment. Because of the security measures, people assume that anyone they see inside their development belongs there. Neighbors may not know one another, but they can still expect anyone they come in contact with to be "one of them." Many of our respondents said that this limited sense of neighboring is adequate for the leisure compound. The perception is that people behind the gates, especially in Blackhawk and similar club-style developments, are part of the same socioeconomic group. Trust, one of the bases of the good community we all dream of, may therefore be easier to find behind gates than outside them.

One can also find happiness and neighborliness behind guard gates. In most gated communities we found the residents generally satisfied with the organization and social presentation of their gated community. Our focus groups and interviews indicate that lifestyle homogeneity is achieved. At the same time, our research suggests that the sense of community that exists is ephemeral, based on common interests and income levels. The community members do not feel strong commitments to one another. They share their living space because they share individual rather than community goals. The retirement, golf and leisure, and new town gated communities are artificial creations, faux communities. They are contrived rather than organic communities in every respect, but they nevertheless meet most of their inhabitants' needs.

The communities people live in exist on many levels: the block, the neighborhood, the town or city, the region, the nation. Some of the lifestyle community residents claim that their safe home ground and organized homeowner associations give them more opportunities to engage with the community beyond their gates than they would otherwise have time for. Others charge that they can and do more easily ignore the world outside. The reality is more complex than either of these views.

As a senior city staff member in Rancho Mirage describes it:

> I work in a community which has at least 60 percent of its residents behind gates. . . . Gated communities have a homogeneous character, they have a reason for people to interrelate, they have elected leadership that take it upon themselves to be very actively involved. I must have two dozen homeowner associations that I must respond to daily who have agendas, who come to meetings. I find them a formidable group of people that have more demands on the government than the open neighborhoods.[12]

He attributes this involvement partly to fear of crime and partly to their economic investment. Despite their activity and organization, the residents rarely form coalitions among themselves. Their interests are their own.

A political leader from the neighboring city of Palm Springs expressed a slightly different take on the civic-mindedness of the gated communities:

> The reason for the activism in Rancho Mirage and Indian Wells is the residents are rich and used to having their voices heard, and they are retired and have time. Also, the gated community has a stronger investment in expressing their needs because they identify with that community. Neighborhoods would have drawn that kind of allegiance in the past. There has been a sense of belonging and of shared destiny between an individual and where they live throughout history which has been lost. The gated community replaces that. I'm wondering if they aren't a market response to that desire for belonging. . . . The gate and the homogeneity reinforces a feeling of shared destiny and [shared interest in] property values.[13]

We heard conflicting reports about whether the citizens of lifestyle gated communities were more or less likely to participate in the wider community than anyone else—but because they live in gated enclaves, with private recreation, roads, parks, and security, they have less need to participate. As the chamber of commerce president in Palm Springs told us, "I've found that the gated community puts you further away from the community itself. You've lost a little of the relationship between what occurs behind the gates and what occurs in the greater community."[14]

Lifestyle developments are meant to provide an ideal base for community connections. In the case of Canyon Lake, these connections are fed through active resident management. In Blackhawk, they spring up around the golf course and tennis club. At Mission Hills, the activities and amenities revolve around the common interests of seniors. Each development type presents its rationale for community differently. In each, the gate adds to the feeling of belonging and security and perhaps even of exclusivity. It shelters and protects the lifestyle within, completing the package of amenities.

Clearly, common interest in property values and community lifestyle should not be discouraged. But are gates required? There are many means of achieving communal connections and a degree of safety. Security systems, walls, and gates provide a means to create association and to protect one's home and real estate investment, but they also separate and exclude, and can present a barrier to wider communalism.

4

I Have a Dream

The Prestige Communities

IN THE GATED prestige developments, commonality is based almost entirely on economic class and status. These developments are rooted in the late nineteenth century, when the richest citizens and the barons of industry attempted to seal themselves off from the hoi polloi. One of the earliest prestige developments was the suburb of Tuxedo Park, built in 1885 behind gates and barbed wire, an hour by train from New York. Tuxedo Park was designed with wooded lake views, an "admirable entrance," a homeowner association "to control the social fabric and the character of the architecture," a village outside the gates to house the servants, and merchants in the village to serve the development.[1] In the same period, private gated streets were built in St. Louis and other cities for the mansions of the rich.

Now the merely affluent, the top fifth of Americans, and even many of the middle class can also have barriers between themselves and everyone else as a sign of their joining the ranks of a new separate—but never equal—American elite.

Prestige communities feed on exclusion and on the status aspira-

74

tions of the well-to-do and upwardly mobile. As in the lifestyle communities, their gates are built by the developers, not by the residents. But prestige communities lack the extensive recreational amenities and services of lifestyle communities; they are generally simple residential subdivisions. We divide them into three types, by income level. First are the enclaves of the rich and famous, those at the extreme top of the income scale; next are the top-fifth developments, for the affluent; and last are the executive developments, for the middle class. All present carefully controlled aesthetics and image and many boast enviable landscapes and locations. Some include lakes or nature preserves; some are designed to take advantage of riverside or oceanside sites. Except in the oldest developments, the prestige communities tend to have ostentatious entrances and showy facades throughout the settlement. Frequently, guards at the gate or roving patrols add to the aura of exclusivity. Residents may value the simple presence of a security force more than the service they actually provide. In the prestige communities, image is of primary importance; their gates denote a barrier of status.

Status is important to most people—working class, middle class, and affluent. The differences lie in what status symbols are valued and accessible. Among households that earn more than $100,000 a year, living in an exclusive neighborhood is a symbol of status or achievement for nearly half; among the very wealthy, who earn more than $400,000 a year, living in an exclusive neighborhood is important to nearly 60 percent (see figure 4-1).[2]

But prestige and markers of status are not the only reason the affluent and the upwardly mobile middle class are choosing gated communities. Gated communities also provide privacy and protection from solicitors and strangers and relief from the fear of crime. In a society in which a heightened fear of crime is changing behavior patterns, the growing popularity of gates is no surprise. One developer in south Florida told us that 90 percent of the housing now under construction is behind some kind of gate. As he says, "People are a little neurotic. [Those] who have suffered from crime or know someone who has are sitting there all day like Chicken Little waiting for the sky to fall in."[3] But the families of the prestige communities can afford to live in neighborhoods where crime is minimal, with or without gates. Even without any credible threat of victimization, gates help assuage the amorphous fear of random crime.

Figure 4-1. *Symbols of Success: Things Considered Status Symbols by American Households of $100,000+ Income and $400,000+ Income*

Percent

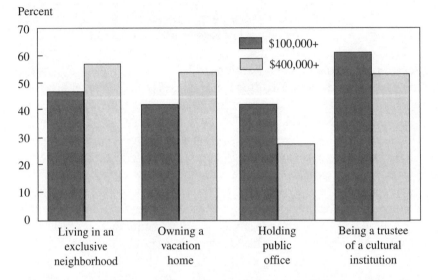

Source: *Town and Country*, "Wealth in America: A Study of Values and Attitudes Among the Wealthy Today," 1994.

One real estate professional told us that his clients were concerned most about protecting their property values. The security comes from similarity in makeup of their neighbors and in the houses in a development. And because his clients tend to travel a lot, the security provided by gates appeals to them.[4] Long hours, dual-career couples, and frequent business and vacation travel mean that their homes, their major investment, stand empty for long periods of time. Gates and guards provide a reassurance, often false, that their property is protected during their absence and that their shared territory is safe. They also provide privacy, block traffic, bar solicitors, and help to create an extra layer of control and separation around their homes.

The Rich and Famous and the Simply Rich

The earliest nonmilitary gated communities in the United States were the walled compounds of celebrities and the very rich. Those elite developments offered residents prestige and privacy by physically separating them from their surroundings, barring entry to all but the privileged and their guests. They included the Florida vacation compounds of the East Coast aristocracy and the neighborhoods of Hollywood stars around Los Angeles. Newer enclaves for the rich and famous, however, are emerging at a rapid pace. There are at least 10,000 professional athletes earning more than $1 million per year. Add to these thousands of other new millionaires created in the 1980s and 1990s on Wall Street and in the high-tech industries, entertainment, law, and major corporations. These nouveau riche are anything but bashful about their resources. Moreover, they live in many regions. Wealth that used to be concentrated around New York City and Los Angeles has spread to Denver, Dallas, Minneapolis, San Jose, Atlanta, Miami, and many other large and small places around the country.

Hidden Hills, near Ventura in southern California, is home to movie stars and celebrities such as Beau Bridges, Tony Orlando, and Bob Eubanks. An incorporated town since 1961, it has moved its city hall outside the gates so outsiders who have business with the city do not actually enter it. Town council meetings are broadcast to each home on the closed-circuit security video system. Hidden Hills has been under court order to provide low-income housing according to state law, but it has been resisting, even to the point of rejecting a nonprofit senior development. The low-income housing battle, among other things, has attracted quite a lot of press for Hidden Hills, and some residents say they don't understand the criticism. A candidate for mayor asked, "Why is it that it leaves such a bad taste in people's mouths just because you have a community of people in expensive houses who just want to close themselves off from all the crime and the rest of it in the city at large?"[5]

One of the major developers of exclusive gated communities in the Dallas, Texas, area defended high-end enclosures: "The number one issue as I see it is that people want a sense of community. I think that is more what the gate is about, more so than security. The security aspect is part of it, but the main thing is 'I want a small town atmosphere in my big city. I want to be part of a community where I can be friends with all these people who are similar to my background.'"

The small, very wealthy settlements composed entirely of the richest and most famous are impenetrable to outsiders, even researchers. The following vignette, however, is illustrative of the upper crust of

A community for the rich and famous: Indian Wells, California

prestige gated communities, where residents are mainly national and local celebrities and top corporate executives.

Our Crowd, Our Town: Cottonwood Valley, Irving, Texas

Cottonwood Valley is one of several gated subdivisions in Las Colinas, a new town in Irving, Texas. Irving is not a rich suburb; its median income of $31,800 is only $4,500 higher than that of the county of Dallas, which it borders, and just $1,700 higher than the national median. Cottonwood Valley, however, is a wealthy hilltop subdivision where an elaborate, twenty-four-hour gatehouse guards about 300 homes. The houses are all very large, dramatic, and imposing, each custom built in different architectural styles. The effect is a bit disconcerting, with modern Southwest stucco next to New England brick; but it also makes clear that here live people who are too wealthy to accept just any suburban tract. Cottonwood Valley is home to a handful of professional athletes and other celebrities, but most residents are not famous, and many are not averse to dropping the names of their well-known neighbors.

We met one evening with a group of Cottonwood Valley residents in the spacious living room of a sprawling brick house. Most were empty nesters. Some were dual-career couples, some not, and most worked as senior executives for large corporations. They were confident, articulate, well dressed, and clearly affluent—nearly all, both men and women, were wearing diamond jewelry. They were a very involved group; all nine were either past or current members of the homeowner association board.

Most had not chosen Cottonwood Valley and Las Colinas for the gates but for the convenient location near the airport, the dramatic homes, or the expectation of secure property values through strict covenants, conditions, and restrictions (CC&Rs). Others wanted the prestige of famous neighbors and an exclusive, wealthy neighborhood. Nonetheless, all said that they appreciated having the gates.

Half the couples in the room had previously lived in gated communities in Dallas and elsewhere. One young couple, Beth and Jim, both lawyers, had lived in a gated community in Las Colinas. "We moved away and lived in an ungated community in Austin. We were used to people not being able to come to our door. After that, we said, 'We want to go back to a gated community.' Privacy and security were real important to us."

Others said they weren't looking for a gated community per se but that security was an important issue for them. Most of the residents are successful corporate executives who were transferred to Dallas by their employers and find that the concentration of similar people in Las Colinas makes for neighborliness. As Linda, who works for a major corporation, explained, "In Boston, you're brand new in the community, and they're very nice, but they've all been there for 150 years and it's really tough to be comfortable. It's quite different here. We probably met more people from New England here in Las Colinas in the first year than we ever met in New England."

Those who had never lived in gated communities elsewhere were first exposed to gates when they began shopping for a house in Dallas, and they were not much impressed. Said one, "It never dawned on us. It didn't mean a thing. I don't think I was seeking security." Bill, who has been active on the board, concurred. "All across the country now, there are so many places that have lovely homes, a few condominiums, and golf courses. They may not have a gate, but they're definitely communi-

ties. We've all lived in places like that. So putting the gate up and saying, 'O.K., now your association dues are a little higher' didn't mean
that much."

The experience of living in Cottonwood Valley has changed some
attitudes toward the gates. A spate of murders in affluent North Dallas
made them more aware that they live in a "kind of oasis." Security consciousness has increased, although crime is low in Las Colinas. Juvenile
mischief and vandalism are the only crime-related problems, and violent offenses are almost unheard of.

Dealing with the "Over-the-Wall Crowd"

They are quick to deny that their oasis is isolated, however. Many are
involved in volunteer and civic activities in the surrounding city of Irving, from the symphony to the hospital. At the same time, several say
that their neighbors tend to dissociate themselves from Irving, which is
not nearly as wealthy as Las Colinas and has a sizable minority population. Especially disturbing to Las Colinas residents is the poor reputation of the schools, which are plagued by poor standardized test scores
and a shortage of bilingual teachers.

Everyone in the group is familiar with local school issues, bond
ratings, and tax issues, despite the fact that none have children at home.
They must be interested, they say, because their property values are affected by the health of Irving, and they still are dependent on the city for
fire, police, library, and other services. Despite the knowledge and concern these residents express, they tell us that Cottonwood Valley had a
very low turnout in the last city council election; they claim that Las
Colinas residents are no less or more likely to vote than anyone else.

Cottonwooders are sensitive to charges of exclusion and separation.
Bill says, "I've heard people refer to the 'over-the-wall crowd,' meaning
people outside the gate. There's an attorney here who uses that phrase
all the time. I asked him if he wouldn't do it because it perpetuates the
split between people." Jim says, "I don't want to sound like I just want
to stay inside the wall and separate myself, because you really can't. On
the one hand you want the security and the privacy, but you know you've
got to be part of the larger world. If you go to the store, and you have
someone who can't make change for you because the schools are bad,
you don't want that. We can't just live in here and ignore the outside
world."

The Community Inside

Community inside the development is another issue. Socialization is initiated and maintained by the wives. Making friends and building community are made easier by the fact that as transplants they all have something in common. There are barbecues and Christmas parties sponsored by the homeowner association, and there are coffees for newcomers. Individual streets sometimes hold block parties. Nevertheless, they are all busy people, and the high turnover in the development due to corporate moves means that relationships among neighbors are difficult to develop and maintain.

But community is not really what any of these people wanted most out of their neighborhood. To these residents, all active, concerned, and worried about the future of their city and their country, Cottonwood Valley is an oasis. It offers two crucial ingredients: security and privacy. If neighborliness can also be found, that is all to the good, but a protected personal lifestyle and secure property values are their first concerns.

"As early as '84," Jim the young attorney offered, "I saw gated communities as a thing of the future. I said then, 'If I had money, I'd invest in these type of communities.' I hate to say it, but crime is getting so bad, that's a major concern." And if security is the push into the gated community, privacy is the pull: "We can't keep the telephone from ringing at 6 o'clock at night, but we can keep people from knocking on our door and constantly trying to sell us something. That's part of a gated community."

The Top-Fifth Communities

In southern California and Florida, gated communities for the wealthy are ubiquitous. Elsewhere in the country, they are growing in popularity. Enclaves of expensive homes, sometimes custom built, are fenced off from their surroundings and marketed for their privacy and prestige. These developments are often smaller than those for the less affluent, sometimes with only a dozen houses, although some incorporate hundreds of units. Security guards often serve the function of concierge, providing notification of arriving guests, admitting housekeepers and

A top-fifth community in Laguna Niguel, California

gardeners, and accepting deliveries. Marketing brochures and advertisements rarely mention gates specifically. Code words such as "private" and "exclusive" are found over and over again.

In affluent Pacific Palisades, located on wooded slopes above the ocean north of Los Angeles, gated communities are common. A resident of one of the newer developments noted, "We knew that [the guardhouse] was going to be here, and it was a factor. It just made it that much more exciting—not only does it give you security but there's a certain amount of prestige that goes with it, too."[6]

Hernando County, near St. Petersburg, Florida, experienced a boom in luxury home construction in the mid-1980s. Doctors, lawyers, and business executives moved into ostentatious gated communities of custom houses. At Waters of Weeki Wachee, a spokesman noted, "The gated entry, the full-time security and the private streets all go along with the pattern and complement the price they pay for their homes." According to a builder specializing in custom homes in the area's gated communities, buyers want houses "that make a clear statement about themselves and their lifestyles."[7]

In the suburbs of Baltimore, gates are becoming more common. Grey Rock is a new development of townhouses and condominiums with a guard gate and a stone and iron fence. The 200 homes inside sell for $134,00 to $260,000. A sales manager for Grey Rock said that the gate shows "we're at a different level, a more upscale community. Any upscale community now would have to be gated. That's what makes it upscale."[8]

The newest of these developments are being built outside of major metropolitan areas in what were once small towns and the outer edges of exurbia—places like Santa Fe, New Mexico, far from the crime and congestion of big-city regions. These new developments are for the "flexexecutives," a group whose numbers are increasing as telecommunications and new forms of corporate structure make smaller organizations the rule rather than the exception. These places must offer this new class of executives considerable charm and visual appeal along with upscale stores, restaurants, and culture and access to outdoor recreation, all, according to Charles Lesser and Company, in a small-town atmosphere.[9]

Whether in the country, the exurbs, or the suburbs, the top fifth of prestige developments serve the growing numbers of professional and senior executives who are well paid, mobile, and status-conscious. In a new town in southern Florida, we found a group of gated subdivision residents who exemplified this trend.

"Paradise, Disneyland, Utopia": Weston, Florida

Weston is a new town on the far outskirts of Ft. Lauderdale, built right on the edge of the Everglades. As in new towns across the country, the streets are wide, the entrance markers monumental, the landscaping lush. Many but not all of its subdivisions are gated. We spoke with residents from three of the gated areas, all very affluent. The group met in the evening in the pool house of one of their subdivisions. They were emblematic of the suburban upper middle class: all white, in their forties and older, and well dressed in chinos, polos, and golf sweaters. Like most successful people, they were used to having their say and being listened to. They were opinionated and articulate, and despite their general agreement they often interrupted and spoke over each other.

All of the residents we spoke to live in guard-gated communities. Unguarded electronic gates in Weston are found only in less well-to-do developments. Despite their seemingly high security, the residents are all realistic about the amount of protection from crime they have obtained by living in a gated community. "One of the things that bothers me is that people tend to take a manned gate as security, as a guard," said one older man, Harry. "He is not a guard, we don't have armed guards, he is strictly someone who is watching unknown vehicles coming in."

But gate guards are eyes on the street for suspicious activities; they can refuse to open the gate to an unauthorized person, and they prevent irritating intrusions by solicitors. One of the neighbors, John, argues, "It is a deterrent to some sorts of people from coming into the community. And you feel better about it. In this day and age, with so much crime, it's just something that helps you feel good about where you live, and a little safer." Out on the farthest edge of suburban Broward County, crime would seem to be a distant worry: the rate of violent crime is one-third that of the metropolitan area, the burglary rate half. But still, anyone can be a victim of crime. John reports that twenty-one robberies occurred in his development in a single two-week period.

Even with gates, guards, and perimeter fences, real security is still out of reach; and these gated community residents reach for ever more security and worry constantly about vulnerability. One development hired an ex-CIA security expert to evaluate their defenses. Because the development backed onto a golf course, the expert said that additional roving patrols would not help and instead recommended a "ninja patrol" that could roam the course in a golf cart with a high-powered spotlight.

The group trades more stories of crime and attempted solutions, but they want us to know that they don't think they are unusual in their fixation on safety. "This is city government. In city government you see this every day." Whether dealt with by a municipal police department or a homeowner association's hired security firm, crime is an issue that unites everyone.

Despite the gates and patrols, security is not what the residents like most about where they live. Mostly they just like Weston. It's beautiful, peaceful, planned, and new. All the residents laud the landscaping, the design, and the fresh and pristine quality of their new town. One of the younger men in the group says, "People bought a marketing concept out here—whatever you want to call it—paradise, Disneyland, utopia." And it is indeed reminiscent of Disneyland: perfectly designed and maintained, every view and experience orchestrated and controlled, with private security to deal with anyone who steps out of line. One half expects to see Disneyland's army of brightly dressed people sweeping up each dropped gum wrapper and fallen leaf.

But Weston is a place to live, not a theme park. Some developments actively try to build community in their fresh new neighborhoods, with pool parties, Halloween parties, Fourth of July parties. But no one claims they have succeeded in creating community. In fact, some subdivisons do not even attempt to plan social activities. One woman who has been active in homeowner association governance explains that many are not looking for a community inside the gates. "Most people I have met already lived in Florida and have most of their friendships and associations outside. We have made friends with our immediate neighbors." Interestingly, in the development that experienced the rash of break-ins, a Neighborhood Watch has been established and social contacts around that effort are beginning to grow.

In all the subdivision homeowner associations, the residents say that participation is limited to a few active and dedicated people and that most residents don't volunteer to help run their neighborhoods. It's difficult to get people to come to meetings. At the same time, Weston has decided to incorporate as a separate municipality, and many of those we spoke to support the move. Their reasons are twofold. First, Weston is a special tax district, established to pay for the new town's infrastructure, and residents believe that incorporation will increase their say over the tax money they pay. "That money is Weston's, and we should control how it's spent." Second, in 2001, the developer, Arvida, will have finished building and withdrawn, and some fear that without the clout of a major corporation lobbying for Weston's interests they will lose power with the county and state governments.

Self-government has its problems in Weston. New residents resist or claim ignorance of restrictions put forth in the CC&Rs. The issues that cause discord can seem trivial—parking, the temperature of the pool, basketball hoops. A major debate is being fought in one subdivision over a five-dollar assessment for planting flowers in the common areas. The issue is so touchy that people begin to shout. The concern is, as always, "taxes." It is also property values, and how far an association should go to protect them against any possibility of falling. Most agreed with the position of one man who lives in a small custom home development. His view: "If we have to force people to keep their real estate values up so you can sell your home at a profit, that's fine."

The Down Side of Gates

Roy Abrams of Weston is the Hollywood image of a young, successful, ambitious lawyer, good looking and passionate about his convictions. But Roy is the real thing—energetic, sincere and charismatic. He ushers us into his office and makes us feel at ease. His office looks like a corporate lawyer's except for two things: his desk is an absolute mess and his walls are covered with letters, convention mementos, and handshake photos from his work with the Democratic Party.

Roy is in his mid-thirties, lives in Weston, and has a law practice with his wife, also a lawyer. They work with gated and nongated homeowner associations and with developers, builders, and banks on subdivision development. Before he came to Florida, he had never seen a gated community. He wanted the security and property value protection he found in the suburban guard-gated community, Weston Hills Country Club, where he now lives.

He knows that some people think living in a gated community smacks of elitism, and he is insulted by the charge. "Does that mean you should be embarrassed that you've worked hard, pulled yourself up by your bootstraps, and done well? Is that elitist, and should I feel guilty about that? I don't. When I go home, I leave part of the outside world behind me. I don't know if there is anything wrong with that. When you go home, it's an inner sanctum, it's a highly protected constitutional right. I should be able to invite those people I want into my home, or my neighborhood or my street. It's a personal thing."

Although happy in his choice to live behind gates, he does see disadvantages. In some ways, they invade the very privacy they are intended to protect. "I am seeing some very sophisticated retrofitting around here, to the point where it's almost an invasion of privacy. Every time you go through with your clicker or your card, the computer has your code, and they know when you're coming and when you're going. Personally, I have nothing to hide, but I don't think it's anyone's goddamn business when I'm coming or when I'm going, and I wouldn't like my neighbors having that information, or the association. I personally would find that offensive."

Furthermore, gates do not guarantee security. There were several break-ins in one area of Weston, all done by a professional thief who simply rode his bike past gate guards. He was white, well dressed, and passed for just another resident. In Roy's own subdivision a thief came in at night by boat through one of the many canals and waterways threading through this area of southern Florida.

"The gate is something of a fallacy," Roy says. "You can always, always penetrate these communities from a number of other locations, across the golf course, with a boat. It doesn't take a mental genius. These communities are not being very well guarded other than the guard gate. Some have roving patrols, but they're really a joke. You see them once every forty-five minutes. Anyone who's done their homework can penetrate one of these communities. I think that guard gates are dangerous to the extent that they create a false sense of security. I always advise people that they ought to realize that the guard gate is not what it feels or seems to be. People have this perception that it's keeping the outside world from coming in."

Just as Roy sees that gates do not automatically grant true privacy and security, he has found that neither have they created true community. "My wife and I just went to the annual Christmas party of the Weston Hills Country Club, and we realized that except for the people we knew, it wasn't this cohesive group of people that you went up to and said hello. I didn't do it and they certainly didn't do it, and we weren't inspired to do it. Interestingly, the neighborhoods sat by tables. It wasn't done on purpose, but people broke themselves down by neighborhood. So our street had two tables. We didn't arrange it. It was really kind of funny."

Execu-burbia: Marblehead, San Clemente, California

When you enter the gated community of Marblehead, you are entering a place of dreams—the dream of Mr. and Mrs. Executive America. They want good schools, nice homes, kids playing in the streets, and friendly neighbors. Marblehead is just that—a nice place to live. It has none of the pretentiousness of the exclusive Palm Springs resorts. The homes, though large, sit on small lots. It is a suburban housing tract of upper-middle-class homes that would look like any other tract anywhere except for the gate and the guard.

We met at the home of Mel, the homeowner association president, on a hilltop with a breathtaking view of the Pacific Ocean and the once sleepy surfing town of San Clemente. He is a big man with a big voice and a kind disposition. In his friendly, forthcoming style, he explains that he ran for the association board to be involved in the group and to have his ideas listened to.

The group that met on Mel's back porch was relatively diverse. There was Ed, a Los Angeles police officer, and the Captain, a retired city official and government consultant. Jim was a longtime resident who also owns a home in Palm Springs. There were Mel's new wife, Barbara, and a retired school teacher from San Clemente named Anna. They knew each other well, because all were or had been active in the subdivision's homeowner association.

They make it clear that Marblehead is no friendlier, no more of a community, not even safer than any other suburban development. "It is just like any other place." Most of these residents seem to have come here by accident, finding the subdivision by chance and buying a home for the ocean views. Mel had lived in a gated community that was guarded and heavily patrolled and didn't like it at all. He purchased his lot in Marblehead because of the views and did not even notice that gates were planned. He was, he admits, "part of the flight from L.A. I hate L.A., I would never live there again." His wife winces at the comment. She starts to say something good about Los Angeles, but Mel stares her down.

Ed, the police officer, found Marblehead while pursuing some bad guys. He had been thinking of leaving the neighborhood he'd lived in for many years, feeling uncomfortable as he began to notice signs of gangs and deterioration. He wanted out, and then he found Marblehead. It wasn't the gate that made Ed feel Marblehead was safer, but its distance from the growing problems he saw everywhere else. "The gate doesn't mean anything," he said. "If the surrounding community has a problem, the gated community has a problem." No one disagrees with him. None feels the gate is a significant feature of the development. It does, they admit, add a touch of prestige to the development, but it really means little. The ocean views are far more important than the gate.

Gates as Status Symbols

This group of residents is not alone among Marblehead residents in de-emphasizing the security of gates. The gate guards are relaxed, really only monitoring and slowing traffic, and no one is willing to pay the cost for improved levels of security. Like nongated communities, the neighborhood has burglaries and other mild vandalism. "We live in a traffic-controlled community, not a secure community," says Jim.

The gates do give the area a prestige that is attractive to new young executives, according to the Captain, but not enough to significantly affect property values. And they do keep solicitors out and prevent some types of easy criminality.

As in most suburban areas, bored teenagers are the major source of crime. But in Marblehead, not all of the problem is internal. There are gangs in San Clemente who have gained access to Marblehead. Ed says, "Gang members come in with the kids that live here; I have seen them. I'll bet the parents did not know they were gang members." A new park being developed just outside the gate is compounding the problem. Teenagers gather there, and some have knocked down the fence between the park and the development to get inside.

Ed says that kids see the gates as "evils that cannot be tolerated." Gates can be an inconvenience to their comings and goings and those of their friends in Marblehead and nearby gated communities. School, sports, friends—all are on the other side of the fence. Gates are a barrier between them and the rest of the world.

Their elders report that they too have more connections outside the gates than within them. Many executives work two to three hours away in downtown San Diego or Los Angeles. Their friendships and community connections likewise are not bound by the territory of Marblehead. Few people have the time to communicate with their neighbors, and few know each other.

Part of the reason for this lack of attachment to Marblehead is the lack of any community center or common gathering area in the development. Jim once tried to get some land from the developer to build a community house, but the developer refused. Because there was little support or enthusiasm for the idea among his neighbors, the idea was dropped.

There are few people who are as involved in the Marblehead home-owner association as Mel. He considers the association an important element in his personal life, but he knows it means little to his neighbors; most feel the need to get involved only when they have something to complain about. The subdivision is composed mostly of "absentee citizens." "They leave when it's dark, they get home when it's dark," says Ed. Thus the association is relatively weak and only a minor presence in Marblehead. There are conflicts about tree heights and other common subdivision disputes, but the hottest issues, which still fail to elicit much participation or interest, are speeding and safety problems due to a lack of stop signs.

Safe Streets

As we cruised through the development in Mel's souped-up pickup, we attracted both the attention and the wrath of a group of young mothers playing with their children on the sidewalk and in the bike lane. "Slow down," they yelled in unison. Mel kept going on the wide street without any appreciable acknowledgment.

When we returned down the same street, Mel alighted from his truck and conversed with the young women. He asked if they would serve on the safety committee. One of the women animatedly said she had been to one of the homeowner meetings and decided that "it doesn't do much." The other women were not eager to volunteer for any new duties. They all said they were already too busy with schools and other commitments. They did not say this with much conviction, but Mel decided not to press. He just said, "If you want to slow down the traffic, you've got to come out."

It seems true that despite the gates the streets of Marblehead are not safe. Because the houses have such small yards, children have to play on the street, but the wide streets were built for speed, not for kids. Anna predicted that "one day someone is going to be killed on these streets."

Nevertheless, the dangers of the Marblehead streets are very different from those of the city streets, which the mothers feared even more. They had not come to this distant, gated, suburban subdivision to escape traffic. But with gangs nearby and crime finding its way through holes in the fence, it may not be long before this little cocoon has the same problems inside the walls as exist outside them. Someone in the group said, "You can run but you can't hide." Mel just smiled.

Executive Communities

Gated residential developments are now available to all of the middle class. They are marketed as "executive" or "professional" communities

An executive gated community: Montecito, Palm Desert, California

by developers, although they are really just standard middle-class sub-divisions. They usually offer no amenities beyond a gated entry, perimeter fence, and perhaps a pool or tennis court. Home to young couples, middle managers, civil servants, and other members of the mainstream middle class, they provide some of the cachet of exclusive living to those with nonexclusive incomes. Many have electronic gates, and others have guardhouses at the main entrance. Sometimes, however, homeowner associations never hire guards because of the high ongoing cost. In those cases, the gatehouse stands as a solely psychological deterrent to outsiders. Individual home security systems are common, and the more sophisticated include video monitors that allow residents to view motorists seeking admittance at the main gate or even to observe the comings and goings of their neighbors by means of cameras placed throughout the development.

In a suburb of St. Louis, University Place was built with just this market segment in mind. A high-density development of 100 townhouses and single-family homes that sold for $170,000 to $235,000 in 1989, University Place has a small green and a toddler playground. In contrast to these modest amenities for the young families the developers hoped to attract, the subdivision's main entrance boasts both a gate and a large monument.[10]

Magdalene Reserve, a small thirty-nine-unit development near Tampa, Florida, won awards for its design, which saved many of the existing trees and left common areas in their natural state. Homes in the subdivision sold for $150,000 to $250,000 in 1991. The woodsy setting is part of the attraction for residents, but so is the entrance gate: "The gate closes in the evening, and you feel free to roam around. People get out and see what their neighbors are doing. It's really friendly."[11]

Executive home developments are very common in southern California as well. One, proposed in 1993 for a valley sixty miles east of San Diego, planned for eighty-four homes on 755 acres, leapfrogging well past existing suburban development. The developer of Stagecoach Springs planned to sell houses with less than 2,000 square feet for $140,000 to $170,000. Stagecoach Springs was designed to be "a very safe community" because of its gates, "an affordable place out in the country for moderate-income families."[12]

Workers can no longer count on a lifelong career in one corporation. Economic restructuring has meant two-income families, multiple employers and positions, and even multiple careers over a lifetime. The new economic reality of the job market is reflected in housing choice. A home must serve both family and business functions. It must offer bearable drives for two wage earners commuting to far-flung workplaces in the metropolitan region. It must be marketable: easily sold and secure from depreciation. And it must offer security for possessions, especially with both adults gone from the house all day. We visited two examples of this sort of moderate-income utopia, one in Florida and one in southern California.

A Family Place: Jacaranda Pointe, Plantation, Florida

Jacaranda Pointe is a 136-unit gated community in a suburb of Ft. Lauderdale. Built in the early 1990s, it is home to young families and a few singles. The homes are modest, resembling homes in any middle-income development with the sole exception that they are behind a security guard arm and an iron fence. The small stucco houses seem all garage, and yet cars are parked in most driveways. The yards are small, and there are few common areas. The group of residents we spoke to were friendly, open, and eager to talk about their development. There was a single man who worked in sales and several couples: a husband who is a police officer and a wife who teaches; a telemarketing entrepreneur and his homemaker wife; two civil servants in downtown Miami. Our host served snacks and sodas as the group straggled in, wearing jeans and looking a bit tired from their day's work. Several had children in tow, who could be heard and occasionally seen playing together in the back of the house.

Jacarandans see their neighborhood as a safer place than most, a place where their kids can play outside without danger from traffic. It should be safer; their suburb, Plantation, has violent crime rates that are two-thirds to half that of the Fort Lauderdale metropolitan area as a whole and a not quite a quarter of Fort Lauderdale's.

Despite the calm of their suburban setting, the positive things these residents say about their development are all related to the benefits of the gate. It makes Jacaranda Pointe quieter and is some deterrent to crime, they think. "I can walk by myself at night." "You wouldn't believe how quiet it is; it's beautiful." "We haven't had any crime at all." In general, though, they were much less bullish about their neighborhood and displayed more ambivalence than most groups we talked to, despite the fact that the problems they mention are no different from those everywhere else.

The gate itself has caused much frustration. It is a relatively low-budget keypad system, and although there is a guardhouse, no guard has ever been hired. The gate is prone to damage from people simply driving through and breaking the arm. Local kids have cut off the power and pulled the phone out, and teenage vandals have shot out the gatehouse windows with BB guns. Still, residents are glad it's there. Especially important to these residents is the effect on traffic. "It might not stop real criminals, but it is going to deter young fellows from going a little fast." To these young families, this is the major benefit, because "our children are at risk."

Self-governance

As in most of the other suburban developments we visited, the topic of rules and regulations instantly generated a heated conversation. The

CC&Rs are seen by some as overly restrictive, arbitrary, or intrusive. With interpretation and enforcement of the rules the main business of the board, it is no surprise that self-government is fraught with complaint and divisiveness. One man reports with disgust, "I dropped out after three or four months because I just couldn't stand the arguing. Nothing was getting done."

He is not alone. Because of lack of participation, all the committees have disbanded. Usually only one person runs for each open board seat. Some have thought of trying to change rules that ban swing sets and basketball hoops but are unsure how to proceed, and the idea has not been pursued. When a resident characterizes the level of involvement among most residents as "active disinterest," no one argues.

A Search for Community

The unhappiest member of the group is a woman from Long Island, who expected this small gated community would be a friendly place where neighbors would be easy to meet. "But I found that people weren't so friendly, they just stayed in their houses. We had different expectations. There was a community pool, and you'd think that with all the people in such a tight area that people would be more bonded together. I don't find that that's been the case. It is a young community, but there's been a lot of nitpicking and arguing."

The neighborliness that exists in the subdivision is among residents of the same cul-de-sac, or people whose children play together, as in many neighborhoods. There have been a few attempts at parties and social events, but the people who attend already know each other through their children's visits to the pool.

The discontented woman wants to move to a small town in the mountains of Utah. One of the civil servants would like to move but doesn't think he can afford it. The rest are happy to stay. They have complaints about the landscape maintenance service, a couple of the neighborhood teenagers, the quality of the new houses, resident apathy, and the difficulties of running the homeowner association, but they anticipate finding the same problems elsewhere. Realistic and pragmatic people, they shrug and note that it's a new subdivision, and besides, "nothing's perfect." However, all admit they'd anticipated a bit more perfection than they got.

Safe Shores: Yacht Haven, Newport Beach, California

Yacht Haven is an older gated subdivision in the Orange County suburbs of Los Angeles. Although it is not on the coast itself, it has a strong
nautical theme—its streets have names like Yacht Winder and Yacht
Harbor. Mr. and Mrs. Dane live in a comfortable, well-appointed home
inside the gates. In their forties, Mr. Dane wears a beard, and Mrs. Dane
is barefoot and wears casual jeans. They have just started a family.

Mr. Dane, who works for a commercial realty firm, has lived here
for seventeen years, when the gated community was first built in 1977.
He says he liked "the layout and the gate, let's face it, for the status
symbol." The twenty-four-hour security was a plus that made the place
special. Mr. Dane speculates that the gate was built not just as a prestige
feature but also as a means of dealing with the major boulevard on the
western border of the development. As he muses about the gate he says,
"We really don't have a guard-gated community, we have a traffic-controlled community."

The Danes doubt that the gate has much weight in the purchasing
decisions of most new residents. In fact, they point out that a larger
nearby development, Harborview, has similar demographics but no
guards or gates at all. However, Mrs. Dane says, Harborview residents
resent the Yacht Haven gates. This ill will extends even to the Harborview
children, who have been known to ostracize Yacht Haven kids.

Mrs. Dane points out that the newest developments she sees are all
guard-gated. "It is the way development is done here," she says. Guard
gates seem to be the product that will sell, even though their own guard
gate, they admit, has had no particularly beneficial effects for them other
than the enhancement of property value potential.

Safety First

A guard is always posted at the main gate, the only official point of
entry. There are other unguarded gates along the major street. These are
intended only for exiting cars, but pedestrians can easily walk through
them. Solicitors, canvassers, and other people sometimes get into the
subdivision that way. Mrs. Dane will not let her kids onto the street
alone because the gates are not really secure. She says they "give an
illusion of safety, but they are really not safe at all." Apparently she is

not alone in this opinion—few children play in the streets without direct parental supervision.

Neighborhood safety is a primary concern for all residents. Mr. Dane recounts a frightening incident that occurred in a nearby gated community with a border porous to pedestrians, just like Yacht Haven. A robbery outside the development went wrong, and the criminals fled into the gated community and took a hostage there. There has been some vandalism within Yacht Haven. Although it has not been serious, it is of enormous neighborhood concern because the perpetrators seem to be insiders. The homeowner association is aware that the main problem in the subdivision is generated by bored youth. But "they are either unable or unwilling to discuss it," Mrs. Dane says.

Currently the development is debating remodeling the gates, but not to install more sophisticated security measures. The proposed remodeling is purely cosmetic, to maintain appearances. Those opposed see little benefit for the money, while the developers and some residents believe the appearance of the gates affects property values.

If there is a community within the walls of Yacht Haven, longtime residents like the Danes would likely be part of it. Yet they feel there is only an economic relationship among these neighbors. The gate doesn't seem to them to help bring people together. There is a swimming pool that brings people together in the summer, but the Danes say, "We see people in the summer at the pool and then don't see them again until next year." The kids don't play together, even those who live close by. As a result, most involvements are through outside associations such as soccer leagues. People meet through play groups, parks, and other means. Their home is just an address.

The development has no place to meet other than the pool. This issue has been the central topic at association meetings in recent years. Some residents recognize that the walls and gate alone can't bind the neighborhood together and want to do more. A park or a recreation center might make a big difference, but there is little real impetus for this. The homeowner association is weak, with little participation or ongoing interest. Mrs. Dane has been to some meetings, but like most subdivision residents everywhere, she attends only when she has specific concerns.

After considerable discussion about what would or would not promote more community in the development Mr. Dane says, "This is a good place to live—it just isn't an interesting place to live."

Community, Crime, and Status

Prestige developments are in many ways the purest form of gated community. Shorn of the extensive recreational amenities of the lifestyle communities, they are exactly what they seem to be from the outside: beautiful homes behind walls, guarded by gates and often sentries. Status symbols, signs that one is doing well, are important to the affluent and those on their way up. When being in the right crowd is an important part of signaling status, gates, with their illusion of exclusivity, are very appealing.

Developer after developer interviewed across the nation confirms that attractiveness and distinctiveness are key attributes in housing for the affluent. The appearance of the subdivision is a large part of the appeal, and the gate creates a positive visual impression. The prestige development residents we spoke to often mentioned the image of their developments, the markers of wealth or even celebrity that they carried.

But image is not all. Despite living in secure, quiet suburbs and upper-class areas, they were concerned about crime and traffic, about noise and inconvenience. While the gate may keep solicitors and other law-abiding citizens from entering, it has little impact on real criminals. Many residents are aware of criminal activity within their neighborhood boundaries, either by teenagers within the development or from outside.

In fact, the wall can be an excellent shield for criminal activity. Police officials differ on their view of gates, but none we spoke to felt they were much of a deterrent. A police captain in Dallas explained that gated communities provide some safety, by restricting access, but they can also hinder law enforcement.[13] For example, some walls and fences cannot be seen through from the street, leaving criminals unobserved by passerby or patrol cars. Often, gates are open during the day for convenience and closed only at night, or guardhouses staffed only after dark, although most residential burglaries happen during the day. Gates provide a false sense of security that encourages lax behavior—doors left unlocked, garage doors left open, alarm systems not turned on. A survey of gated and nongated communities found that homeowner association board members in gated communities were more likely to report open garage doors and gates as problems than were those in nongated communities.[14] In addition, there is always a trade-off between crime defenses and emergency access. Even with an excellent system for fire and medical access, the gate can add crucial seconds to response time. For this reason, a firefighter in Dallas told us he was always opposed to gates, reasoning that the chance of needing life-saving fire or ambulance service is greater than the chance of being burglarized, and the potential cost to life and property is much higher.[15]

Even traffic, that other problem for which gates are supposed to be a panacea, remains an issue in many gated communities. In both Jacaranda Pointe and Marblehead, speeding cars within the gates are a longstanding issue. Mrs. Dane of Yacht Haven believed traffic was no better on the streets inside the gate than outside. She is not alone.

Many of the people we spoke with bemoaned the lack of community in their developments. Squabbles within the association and apathy among residents were cited again and again. The wall seems to bind the residents together, but it does so only physically. When it comes to socializing or governing, the ties between those behind the gate appear to be no stronger than they would be in an otherwise similar but nongated development.

In part, the reasons that drove residents to choose a gated community are themselves barriers to neighboring. Gates provide a sense of security for the property that often is unoccupied because of dual careers, frequent business travel, and long work hours. By the same token, communities take time and work, but many of the residents in prestige gated communities have little time for one another and hardly any time to devote to building a community. As Roy Abrams, the Weston lawyer, and his wife discovered, community cannot be purchased any more than complete physical security. One can buy controlled access, professional management, and yard maintenance; but community—a common bond, interdependence, and meaningful association—cannot be purchased at any price.

5

Enclaves of Fear

Security Zone Communities

THE DRIVE to redefine territory and protect boundaries is being felt in neighborhoods of all income levels throughout America's cities. Much of the growth in gated communities is not created by developers but by residents of existing neighborhoods who install gates and barricades in an attempt to defend their existing way of life. These are the security zone communities, the closed streets of the city, suburb, and barricade perches. We define this type by the origin of its gates and fences: unlike the lifestyle and prestige communities, where gates are built by the developer, in security zone communities the residents build gates and retrofit their neighborhoods with security mechanisms. In the city and suburb perches, residents turn their neighborhoods into gated communities by closing off all access and sometimes hiring guards. In the barricade perches, full closure is impossible, and residents barricade or gate off as many streets as possible to restrict access. The fortress mentality is perhaps clearest here, where groups of people band together to shut out their neighbors.

Poor inner-city neighborhoods and public housing projects use security guards, gates, and fences to keep out drug dealing, prostitution, and drive-by shootings and regain control of their shared territory. Other neighborhoods, frightened by spillover crime from nearby areas or irritated by traffic, have obtained city permission to take their streets out of public use, limiting access to residents only. In the inner suburbs, both near and far from high-crime areas, existing neighborhoods tax themselves to install security gates or petition the government to barricade their streets. Whether crime is rampant or infrequent, the threat actual or perceived, the fear itself is very real.

The national reach of the media, and its insatiable appetite for dramatic human-interest stories, means that a crime committed in a small town in the Pacific Northwest is reported from Seattle to Miami. This dynamic fuels the fear of crime and the dogged perception that crime is worsening—even in periods like the early 1990s, when crime rates actually dropped. Almost 90 percent of Americans think crime has gotten worse, but the violent crime rate in cities dropped 25 percent between 1981 and 1989. And while 55 percent worry about being a victim of crime and the same percentage feels inadequately protected by the police, only 7.4 percent mention crime when asked what bothers them in their neighborhoods.[1]

The seeming randomness of crime is also responsible for this heightened fear. Gangs in the central city more and more affect those outside through carjackings and drive-by shootings. Cities are viewed as the core area of crime. But no one can be certain. Youth and crime are linked in our minds, and minority youth bear a disproportionate burden of this rising fear. But strangers of any description are an automatic inducement to fear and distrust. This is one reason that traffic is of equal or even greater concern to many neighborhoods that close themselves off: in the new equation of social mistrust, traffic is caused by strangers, strangers are bad, and bad means crime.

Realistically, crime is a far greater problem for lower-income people than for the better off. Data from the Bureau of Justice Statistics' National Crime Victimization Survey show that it is also a greater problem in cities than in suburbs or rural areas. The rates of both violent crime and household crime such as burglary are about 35 percent lower in the suburbs than in cities (see table 5-1). City residents are one and a half

Table 5-1. *Personal and Household Crime Rates per 1,000 Population,*[a] *1989*

Type of crime	Center cities	Suburbs	Rural areas
Violent crime	40.6	26.0	21.10
Rape	1.2	0.5	0.04
Robbery	10.0	3.9	2.10
Assault	29.4	21.6	18.70
Personal theft	86.0	70.1	45.10
Household crime	232.1	152.70	120.40
Burglary	79.3	52.20	48.50
Motor vehicle theft	26.7	16.80	6.10

Source: Bureau of Justice Statistics, *National Crime Victimization Survey* (Washington, D.C.: U.S. Department of Justice, 1993).

a. The rates for violent crime and personal theft are per 1,000 people twelve years of age and older. Household crimes are per 1,000 households.

times more likely than suburbanites to be victims of violent crime or household burglary.[2] Plantation, Florida, where Jacaranda Pointe is located, had a crime rate of 95 per 1,000 residents in 1993; the neighboring city of Fort Lauderdale's rate was 171 per 1,000. Blackhawk Country Club's suburb of Danville, California, had a rate of 19 per 1,000, much lower than the San Francisco metropolitan area rate of 73 per 1,000.[3] Yet residents in both developments felt they needed gates. As we have seen, the real danger of crime, or the real threat from traffic, bears no necessary relationship to the fear of crime. In places with high crime rates, places with low crime rates, places where crime is rising, and places where crime is dropping, fear can spur the gating of neighborhoods that were once open to their surroundings.

Fear is real. Whatever the actual threat of crime, fear in and of itself negatively affects families, neighborhoods, and quality of life. It must be addressed. Even where crime is rare, parents no longer let children wait at school bus stops unattended. Everyone has witnessed the ravages of crime in places near to them. Many feel anxious, some even panicky. It is natural and understandable that people want to do whatever they can to insulate themselves from the threat and to relieve their fear.

City Perches

Gates, fences, and walls are no longer reserved solely for the rich. City neighborhoods, from the wealthiest to the most poverty-stricken, are installing gates and fences, completely closing themselves off. Lower-income neighborhoods that gate are desperate to control crime and regain control of their streets. In public housing projects and very low income neighborhoods, government, police and neighborhood residents are banding together to build systems of fences, gates, and security checkpoints to control gang activity, drug dealing, and other crimes. These gates and walls are more often paid for by the city government or the local housing authority than by the residents, but the initiative can come from either. In any case, these walls differ from those discussed so far in that they are seen by their builders as an exigency rather than an amenity.

The higher-income areas that gate for security are often surrounded by or near lower-income, higher-crime areas. These neighborhoods are trying to hold on to their homes and maintain their property values in the face of the growing violence around them. Elsewhere in the city, neighborhoods are gating even when crime is not literally at their doors; rather, they fear its spread, its randomness. New developments throughout cities are now commonly being built with gates already in place. Often they are equally or even more concerned with mitigating the noise, traffic, and other inconveniences of urban life. In all of these situations, the people of the city perches feel their gates to be less a choice than a necessity.

Potomac Gardens is an example of the use of gates in public housing, where residents often are walled off without petitioning for gates themselves or even giving their consent. The June 1992 installation of gates and fences inside and around the Washington, D.C., project initially angered residents. Firefighters arriving to put out protest fires were stoned by the crowd of residents. Comparisons were made to jails and zoos, with residents telling reporters, "It's disrespectful. We aren't animals. We don't need to be caged." The security measures included identification cards, security cameras, and twenty-four-hour guards.[4] The measures dramatically reduced drug dealing and vandalism, however, and the majority of tenants came to support the "Fence" within a few months.[5]

A city perch: Whitley Heights, Los Angeles, California

A resident of Mar Vista Gardens, a forty-three-acre public housing complex in Los Angeles with a similar system of gates and fences, explains that many residents want a gated community for the "same reasons rich people want to live in gated communities—to cut down on crime."[6] Oscar Newman, who has consulted with a number of housing authorities to redesign common spaces, believes that the addition of fences and gates divides large public areas into smaller territories that residents can more easily identify as theirs and so take greater responsibility for. Increased safety, lower crime, and more attention to maintenance result.[7]

There are some who question the wisdom of fencing off public housing projects and poor neighborhoods. According to Mark Baldassare: "These gated communities discourage residents from interacting with the outside world. The wealthy want that, but the poor don't. The poor need to link up with the community outside their walls because they need the jobs, the contacts, the resources. Putting a housing project in a fortress-like setting further stigmatizes the residents."[8]

There is no question that the wealthy city neighborhoods want reduced interaction with the outside world. Gating of urban streets is more common in wealthier, not poorer, neighborhoods. But no matter how privileged the population, when a neighborhood makes an effort to fortify its boundaries, controversy often ensues. That is exactly what happened when the neighborhood of Whitley Heights decided to gate itself off.

We've Seen the Enemy: Whitley Heights, Hollywood, California

The Hollywood Bowl, scene of so many exhibitions of talent, is also the front porch of one of the most panoramic vistas in the Western world. Above the Hollywood Bowl to the north, east, and west is a small range of hills known as the Santa Monica Mountains. The hills and surrounding terrain are reminiscent of the Dalmatian coast of what was Yugoslavia or the Costa Brava of Spain, except that the views are of freeways, houses, and city streets, not the sea. These hills are, in fact, at the geographic heart of Los Angeles, and they may be the symbolic heart of the city of imagination as well. The land makes its own statement and demands a certain type of architectural integrity, and the homes on the hills match the splendor of the natural setting. Each home is unique, as in an Italian village, yet all are integrated by a similar Mediterranean architecture.

Whitley Heights is one of these hill neighborhoods that rise above Hollywood. As a part of old Hollywood, the area has historically been a film and artist colony. Writers have gained inspiration from the views and the pleasant walking areas. Film stars have found small hideaways from their publics. Whitley Heights has only two entrances—one from Hollywood Boulevard on the south and the other from the Hollywood Bowl parking lots on the north. The street pattern is so irregular, steep, and confusing that few drivers venture beyond the first streets. But by the late 1980s the social geography of Hollywood was changing so fast that the natural topography of the streets and hills and the signs of wealth were no longer sufficient to insulate the neighborhood from the streets below.

Today the contrast between the flatlands of Hollywood Boulevard and Whitley Heights could not be greater, despite the few short blocks that separate them. Below are lanes of traffic, billboards, litter, homeless people, and apartment buildings in varying states of repair. Above are winding streets, tall trees, and mansions. Over the years, as Hollywood Boulevard became the site of prostitution, drug dealing, and other urban ills, the people in Whitley Heights began thinking of gates. There was little crime on the hill itself, but fear of the neighboring streets grew. Everyone knew that the Los Angeles Policy Department was overwhelmed by the problems in the flatlands below.

Some in the neighborhood began to feel the need to gate the area as long as fifteen years ago, in the early 1980s, after the murder of two elderly people whose home was at the base of the hill near Hollywood Boulevard. Some form of security enhancement was clearly necessary. Gates were not the only proposal put before the homeowner association meetings; some residents suggested armed patrols, others a better neighborhood patrol or partially blocking some streets to make the area even less hospitable to auto traffic.

No matter how strong the fear and the perception of crime, cars were perhaps an even greater concern to those on the hill. Because few of the apartment buildings at the bottom of the hill had sufficient parking for their tenants, and the streets on Whitley Heights were safer, the apartment residents were parking their vehicles on the hill. By the early 1980s, commuters had discovered that the hill was a convenient shortcut when the freeways were jammed with cars. Residents noticed more speeding traffic and feared for the safety of their children. There had even been a few high-speed police chases through their tree-lined streets. As more and more people discovered the beauty and charm of the area, more outsiders came to use it as a shortcut, as a jogging area and dog run, and as a cheap parking spot for Hollywood Bowl events.

In 1986 a decision was made to install iron gates, and the city council approved the plan.

Resisting Gates

Bob McDowall was president of the Whitley Heights Civic Association during the period when the final plan to gate was born. He is a man of medium build with strong shoulders, an open and engaging personality, and a touch of an English accent. He told the story of the Whitley Heights gates from the porch of his home, overlooking an Italian garden with a mixture of vegetables, flowers, and water fountains.

Bob came to Whitley Heights in 1989 from New York. He found the area by chance, and immediately appreciated its charm and the beauty of its architecture. He felt that Whitley Heights was a real community, with a sense of history and shared destiny and a strong neighborhood organization. It held an annual Labor Day street festival and an auction to raise money for it.

It was this community that the gates were meant to protect. "Gating was not propelled by any high increase in crime, but a sense that we could not control our community," explains Bob. The gates were seen primarily as a traffic measure, designed to control "who got up here." They were very strongly supported by the residents, with over 80 percent voting in favor. Only one person, a lawyer, vocally opposed the plan, and rather than live in a gated community he moved out. No one else followed his lead.

The fund-raising for the gates was complete by 1988, and in 1990 Whitley Heights received permits to build the gates and withdraw its streets from public use. Early the following year, when construction began, opposition emerged from the neighbors in the apartment buildings on the other side of the new gate. Calling themselves CAGE, the Citizens against Gated Enclaves, they energetically fought the gates. A lawsuit was filed, and the dispute became the center of hot citywide debates over street closures. CAGE charged that the gates were an exclusionary, elitist slap in the face; Bob claims they were just upset that they would lose their parking spaces.

Shortly after construction began, it was discovered that the fire department had never approved the gate plan, and the work was halted. The Whitley Heights Civic Association was forced to redesign the gates to allow for emergency vehicle access. The changes cost $100,000, bringing the total expense to $350,000. Even when completed, the gates stood open, hostage to the lawsuit making its way through appeals. Finally, in June 1994, the California Supreme Court let stand the decision of the appellate court. The gates to Whitley Heights were illegal and could never be closed.

The decision, based on the California Vehicle Code, held that public streets must remain accessible to the public. Wrote Judge Woods of the State Court of Appeals, "Although we understand the deep and abiding concern with crime prevention and historic preservation, we doubt the Legislature wants to permit a return to feudal times with each suburb being a fiefdom to which other citizens of the State are denied the fundamental right to access to use public streets within those areas."[9] CAGE had won. In October 1994, Whitley Heights reached a settlement with the city to split the cost of removing the gates and patching the street and sidewalks.

The Death of Community

The stress of the three-year gating fight exhausted the Whitley Heights community. There was constant fund-raising to pay attorneys' fees and to redesign the gate. Internal conflicts erupted over how or even why to pursue the case. Frustration was heightened by the perception that the city had led the neighborhood astray and was giving in to a small group of radicals. For the first time since 1924, when the Whitley Heights Civic Association was formed, the community auction was canceled, and neither it nor the Labor Day street party has been held since.

Even before the end of the exhausting struggle, the neighborhood association board collapsed and the leadership dissolved. Whereas it had formerly been an active force in political and social issues in Hollywood, a crucible for democratic leadership, and an ally of area charities, now it withdrew. To Bob, Whitley Heights had been the healthy cell of the city of Hollywood. Neighborhoods like Whitley Heights, "when they stay healthy and viable and active within the community, can begin the process of turning around a community that is decaying politically and socially," he explained. For Bob, the battle over the gates ended all chance of that, having deep and lasting consequences for the entire Hollywood area. The community did begin to reform itself with a new neighborhood association composed of newcomers. Nevertheless, the lawsuit was a draining process; even if the neighborhood had won, it would have been a Pyrrhic victory.

The gates would have been an administrative nightmare anyway, Bob says now. "The gate itself was a financial albatross." The board wanted to propose that the gates remain open during the day and closed at night so that deliveries could be made easily. They were even willing to let the flatlanders park in certain locations. But an out-of-court settlement was never really possible. To those on the hill, the fight was to save their community. To those on the flatlands, the fight was to keep the hill dwellers from dividing Hollywood with fences. In the process, Whitley Heights may have lost its most precious resource, its sense of self as a strong community. Bob certainly sees it that way; he moved away shortly after our interview. But on that evening, sitting looking out at the sun fading behind the hills, his loss was plain in the tears in his eyes.

Suburb Perches

Middle-class homeowners in inner-ring suburbs and smaller cities are also turning to gates. They may be fearful of high crime rates in nearby neighborhoods or simply afraid that the demographic change and growing violence around them could one day be at their doors. In so many cases, dramatic changes are already transforming their once peaceful and homogeneous inner-ring suburbs. Many believe they have only two possible responses: move further out or gate their neighborhoods in a last attempt to cling to their place in the social and economic hierarchy.

In the suburbs of New York, Los Angeles, Washington, D.C., Chicago, Miami, Atlanta, and other cities, subdivisions composed of single-family houses and townhouses are gating, especially those developed with private streets, a homeowner association, and only one or two entrances. At such developments, gating is as simple as a vote by the association, an extra assessment, and the installation of the hardware. In the suburbs of Fort Lauderdale, the Boulevard Woods North subdivision began planning to gate after a young woman in the neighborhood was abducted and raped. The residents acknowledge that it is not a high-crime area, but they wanted to do what they could to keep it safe.[10] In Seal Beach, another Orange County suburb, the development of College Park West turned to gates as the answer to a growing problem with crime and transients spilling over from Long Beach.[11] And in Thousand Oaks, a well-to-do suburb of Los Angeles, the residents of Braemer Gardens gated their townhouse development to maintain their peaceful neighborhood and deter crime.[12] Hidden Valley, in southern California, went so far as to spend $50,000 on an electronic antiterrorist bollard of the type used to protect embassies and the vice president's mansion. The device has impaled several vehicles that attempted to enter without authorization.[13]

Whatever the fears and stresses that lead a neighborhood to gate, the end goal is control. Fear comes from a feeling of powerlessness and vulnerability. Gating, as an attempt to exercise control over the environment, lessens that feeling, irrespective of the reality of the threat or the actual effectiveness of the gates.

A suburb perch: Bermuda Dunes, California

Outside Chicago, the suburb of Rosemont has taken the gating trend to a new extreme. The village of 4,000 has installed gated checkpoints at the two entrances to its largest residential area. Staffed by city police and paid for from city coffers, the guardhouses and gates allow police to record license plate numbers and entry times and question drivers. The few crimes that occur in Rosemont usually take place in a commercial area of freeway-exit hotels and businesses that serve nearby O'Hare Airport, not in the residential area; but the crimes are what prompted the gating. Residents fear the flow of strangers. Interestingly, almost half of Rosemont's citizens live outside these protective gates in three apartment buildings. The city claims that including the lower-income renters in the taxpayer-provided secure area would be too costly.[14]

Sometimes crime is not even an issue for a gating. In the wealthy, exclusive Brentwood district of Los Angeles, residents of the Brentwood Circle neighborhood gained permission to privatize their streets, install fences, and build a twenty-four-hour guarded entry.[15] The primary concern was the potentially increased traffic from a new museum being built on a hill directly above them. No streets in Brentwood Circle lead to the museum, but residents feared visitors would assume they did. Of course, the gates are also expected to increase security, privacy, and property values. Said one resident, "We're delighted. Everyone who gets lost (on Sunset) comes up here. The guards at the gate will keep out the riffraff."[16] Not everyone in Brentwood Circle would agree with that inflammatory statement, of course. As in other suburb perches, they simply want to preserve the neighborhood as they know it.

Not Far Enough Away: Sunrise Palms, Palm Springs, California

The image of Palm Springs is that of a rich desert resort, untouched by the cares of the rest of the country. In fact, it is just one of a series of small contiguous cities in the Coachella Valley, home to the rich and famous but also to farm workers, trailer park residents, and all the troubles that come with poverty. Palm Springs has rates of murder, rape, and aggravated assault just slightly higher than its metro area, which itself has rates slightly higher than the nation's. The burglary rate is 50 percent higher than in the Riverside metro area. A city of just 41,000 people, it had seven murders in 1993.

Sunrise Palms is a modest development of 360 clustered attached homes on the north side of Palm Springs. A little past the electronically controlled gate, where a visitor phones in for admittance, there is a tennis court, a pool, and a park area. A small building beside the courts is used as the property manager's office and as a meeting space for the homeowner association. It was in this building that we met eight residents and the resident property manager to talk about life in their working- to middle-class gated community.

When we arrived, the manager had made coffee for the group, most of whom were already there. They sat around a long table in plastic deck chairs, talking animatedly and joking with each other and the property manager. No introductions were needed with these neighbors; they knew each other well. Almost all were older than fifty, but the group was otherwise diverse: men, women, two expatriate Europeans, and a Latino.

Retrofitting for Peace of Mind

Sunrise Palms was not always gated. Built in 1983, it did not have gates until 1991. The movement to gate was supported by 200 of the 360 homeowners; those opposed resisted the cost of installation and ongoing maintenance. The residents were worried about crime, what they saw as the random nature of attacks. They were concerned that as Palm Springs grew they would be overwhelmed by traffic and left vulnerable to criminals. Gating the two entrances to their subdivision seemed like an ideal way to preserve their quality of life.

The gate system itself was carefully chosen. More advanced than the average unguarded electronic gate, it uses magnetic cards and a computer to track who enters and when. Visitors are buzzed through after calling their intended destination, and these entries are likewise tracked. Outsiders who need to come in frequently, from newspaper deliverers to gardeners, are issued vendor cards. The vendor cards work only on the rear gate, which cannot be opened from 10 P.M. to 7 A.M. At both entrances, there is an iron gate that rolls back and also an arm that raises and lowers. The first prevents pedestrian as well as vehicle access, and the second prevents an unauthorized car from driving in after another goes through. We had never seen this double-gating before, and apparently neither had most of the local tradespeople, several of whom were caught under the arm when trying to tailgate during the first few months after its installation.

Other problems occurred in the first months after the gating. Packs of teenagers would wait by the gate, running through behind a car to weekend night parties. There are fewer parties now. Also, some cars tried to drive in through the exit gate, and kids on bikes rode through. As the area around has grown used to the streets being shut off, the problems have diminished. A guard would obviate these problems, but the cost is too high. Most of the residents we talked to had moved in before the gating, but all residents in the focus group were very positive about it. "It's a boon if you're a widow or a widower. I am not as apprehensive here coming into my house, it's a lot more safe feeling." "Before it was gated, I had to keep everything locked. There were transients coming through, walking up and down the street. You can't question them, 'what are you doing here?' because these are public streets, or they were. "Now it's a good secure feeling."

Everyone in the group had experienced break-ins or robberies in the past, and several minutes are spent telling stories of past crimes. They feel that there is a real increase in security with the gates, not just a psychological effect. Most significant, traffic has dropped by 75 percent, and that alone means fewer strangers. Nonetheless, the fence can be jumped, as one woman points out. "Two Mexicans have been coming to the park around 11 o'clock at night to drink beer by the pool." The property manager hadn't heard of this, though it had been going on for nearly a week. She promises to watch for them tonight and call the police (this development has no roving patrol or guards). She notes that no development can promise "security," to which one man responds that there are "federal prisons they call maximum security and they break out of there!"

Community Participation

About 60 percent of the units are second homes, with the remainder divided between full-time renters and owners. This group of residents is similarly mixed, and all want us to know that they are welcoming and accommodating to all who live in Sunrise Palms, even if only for part of the year. Renters are consciously integrated into the homeowner association, despite the fact that they have no legal rights in the governance of the development. An informal attempt is made to keep renters and part-timers represented on the board with full-time resident homeowners.

This effort speaks of a level of involvement in community affairs that is far from the norm for homeowner associations. In fact, the annual elections garner 80 to 90 percent participation; the annual meeting must be held at a local hotel to accommodate all who attend. There is no problem filling board seats, and most slots are contested, which is also unusual for a homeowner association.

The level of involvement is high, but it does not necessarily mean unity within the development. There is now an effort under way to raise the masonry walls surrounding Sunrise Palms on the street sides. On the interior sides, a thirteen-year-old fence is in need of replacement. When assessments for the wooden fence and the outside wall came up for vote, the results were split: those near the outside voted to raise the masonry wall but not to replace the interior fence. Those near the inside voted the reverse.

Issues like this are dealt with through the development newsletter and by committees, although most of the committees have ceased to exist owing to lack of participation. The disaster committee is active, as is a chapter of the Jaycees. The rest of the committees—the pool, architecture, and beautification committees—dissolved because "it's hard to tell your neighbor that they should change something." They all prefer to leave such "enforcement, judge, and jury" duty to the property manager.

This curious mix of involvement and avoidance is also seen in their relationship to the city of Palm Springs. These residents do not feel particularly attached to the city of which they are part, but they do not simply ignore it. "I don't think we take a great interest in it, but I'd be willing to bet that our participation is greater here than where we were from. We're more concerned and more caring." Perhaps because of the high proportion of retirees, many volunteer. All of the women present volunteer at literacy programs, museums, or hospitals, and all of the men say that their wives do as well.

At the same time, political activity inside the gates is effectively banned, just as it is in most homeowner associations. Door-to-door canvassing and the display of signs are prohibited. The group views such activities as divisive, leading to arguments or even fights when the cause is political, and as an annoyance when commercial. Sale of Girl Scout cookies and candy to support the school band is officially prohibited but goes on anyway because no one has any real objection. Canvassing is also a security concern: strangers may be criminals, and flyers left on doorknobs or stoops can be an indication of an empty house.

Neighborliness

The mention of these dangers leads the group to insist that they do watch out for each other and would pick up mail and papers for an absent neighbor. In fact, the subdivision has one invalid who is helped by more than a dozen people. Again, they claim that there is more togetherness here than in a public street neighborhood. "We know about it [neighbors' needs] because we talk to each other, more than on a public street."

"I think the things we're talking about here, it's because it's a homeowner association. In any homeowner association I think you'd have more community spirit than just on a block." No one feels any real change in community feeling since the gating—the pool was busier before, even late at night, but on the other hand now there's a communitywide effort at holiday lighting for Christmas.

One resident contributes, "I guess the gates make it a family." Everyone laughs but agrees. Because of the gates, "you can tell someone who doesn't belong here." Outsiders used to come in and use the park, and no one could ever be sure if they were neighbors or not. Now, with the gate, it's easier to get to know the faces. Although the part-timers are known less well, everyone says they are aware when someone returns in the winter. This issue of belonging is slightly sensitive: the locks on the pool and the tennis courts are scheduled to be changed because former residents sometimes come back to use the facilities.

There are occasional clashes between individuals over parking, noise, or unleashed dogs, but these are not considered frequent or significant. This relative peace is maintained because, as one woman explained, "If we lived on a block outside, and we had a disagreement, we would never get together, because we'd never see each other. Here we see each other. You make an effort that you're not going to let it get at you." Another woman agrees, "If you lived at opposite ends of (an open) street, you could just go in opposite directions." They think the gate itself may help enforce this friendliness. They must know each other, engage with each other, and so they look out for each other and even take care of each other. One of the men says, "We disagree quite a bit on a lot of issues, and yet we're friends." As an example, he says that he when he makes a trip to buy fresh farm eggs for himself, he also buys them for several other people, including some in the room. They smile in acknowledgment.

Like other subdivisions everywhere, gated and nongated, there are problems. Conflicts sometimes arise between neighbors. But the residents of Sunrise Palms, having chosen to circle their wagons against the noise, traffic, and crime of the outside world, know that they need to care for the community within that circle.

Barricade Perches

As the middle-class homeowners of older urban and inner suburban neighborhoods seek to protect their investments, they are turning not just to hired security patrols and Neighborhood Watch groups but to barricades and iron gates that block access to their streets. The complete closure of all entrances to a neighborhood by fences and gates is usually not possible. Where streets are public, legal troubles like those encountered by the Whitley Heights neighborhood often follow. Public streets can be privatized, but the expense is often more than either residents or the city is willing to bear. The tactic in such city neighborhoods is usu-

A barricade perch: Miami Shores, Florida

ally to barricade streets, closing the majority of intersections and leaving just one or two points of entry. The effect is to create the suburban cul-de-sac pattern of a maze of dead-end streets out of the open city grid. These are the barricade perches. Like the other security zone types, they are created by resident, rather than developer, initiative.

Although they are not completely walled or fenced and their entrances are not guarded with gates, we include them because they come as close as possible to gating, and because their intentions to privatize and exclude are the same. And like the other forms discussed in this book, barricade perches are intentionally designed security settlements with restricted access to normally public spaces. The effect is as close to full gating as is practicable. In Miami, Houston, and other cities, dozens of neighborhoods have turned to this solution. In some there are long backlogs of neighborhoods waiting for approval of plans to barricade.

We visited streets that have been closed in Los Angeles, Miami, Dallas, and Palm Springs; and there are similar movements in cities across the country, including Chicago, New Orleans, Houston, Fort Worth, Boston, and Bridgeport, Connecticut. The list grows every year. In

Florida, the state's Safe Neighborhood Act allows neighborhoods to negotiate with their local governments to close, privatize, or modify the right-of-way on public streets.[17]

Reasons range from gangs and other pressing crime problems on their own streets to spillover crime, traffic congestion, commuters using their streets as shortcuts, and general safety from the amorphous threats of disorder in the city as a whole. Proponents support street closures as an effective crime deterrent that helps maintain neighborhoods and homeownership levels and helps curb white and middle-class flight to the suburbs.

Franklin Villa in Sacramento, California, is a low-income neighborhood of apartment and condominium complexes that has serious problems with gangs, drugs, and violent crime. In 1993, after years of demands by neighborhood residents, the city agreed to barricade streets into the neighborhood as part of a $2.3 million community revitalization plan.[18] Because of the Whitley Heights case, these barriers, like any attempted on private streets in California, were temporary. While they lasted, they were welcome. Before that, individual complexes had attempted to control crime on their own; one homeowner association spent more than $200,000 on an iron fence and security guards who patrolled with guns and dogs.[19]

Athens Heights, a working- to middle-class neighborhood in South Central Los Angeles, is just a few blocks from Normandy and Florence, the epicenter of the L.A. riots. It contains some grand old houses and more modest stucco bungalows, most built in the 1950s, all with carefully tended lawns and gardens. Surrounding the neighborhood are some of the poorest, most crime-plagued blocks in Los Angeles. Athens Heights homeowners began seeking approval to gate their streets in 1987 and finally installed one permanent iron gate and several temporary wooden barricades in 1991. The original plan called for ten iron gates, leaving only a single open street into the neighborhood. Residents say crime decreased after the gating. A resident of Athens Heights, noting the isolation and loss of community the gates have brought, said, "The children going back and forth to school, the way that they now have to go [they see] a lot of graffiti, and I think if they walked through here, they'd see a lot of beauty instead. It's regrettable that they're now precluded from seeing that, and there's nothing like seeing a child growing up and going to school. Hopefully, one of these days, we'll be able to allow the children to return."[20] By 1994, because of the Whitley Heights decision, the barricades were down.

As in Whitley Heights, street closures often generate vocal opposition. In the Hillcrest area of Maplewood, New Jersey, five wrought-iron gates were installed in 1993, to the outrage of neighboring Newark. As in many of these street closure battles, the Hillcrest homeowner association steadfastly maintains that it simply wants to reduce through-traffic on residential streets. Hillcrest residents are middle-class professionals, and about half of them are black. The section of Newark with which they share a border is a poor, run-down neighborhood. The Hillcrest residents want what the suburbs have, the cul-de-sac street layout that they say planners have decided is preferred to the urban grid that their homes were built on. Mayor Sharpe James of Newark went on a round of radio and television talk shows denouncing Hillcrest's "elitist" and "destructive" gates. The issue to James is "class separation," which will "cause divisiveness instead of cooperation." The NAACP became involved in the dispute, taking a "proactive stance" against the growing trend of gated communities and neighborhoods barricading their streets.

The Five Oaks neighborhood near downtown Dayton, Ohio, was struggling with growing through-traffic from commuters, problems with prostitution and drugs, and the flight of longtime residents. The city's answer was a 1992 plan to gate off streets throughout the neighborhood, creating eight mini-neighborhoods of three or four streets each. Each mini-neighborhood has only one entrance point, the rest of the internal streets being closed with automatic gates. None of the feeder streets are continuous from one border to another. While the closure of streets was intended to reduce crime and traffic, it was also meant to clearly define the mini-neighborhood streets as being under the control of its residents. "It would evoke proprietary feeling by residents. The nature of the streets would change from open, public thoroughfares without any association or defined identity, to closed, limited access streets with which residents identify and to which they bring their own character."[21] The closure of the streets of Five Oaks has been deemed a success by the police and most of the residents, although some continue to oppose it. Crime is down, and property values have risen.[22] And as cities across the country fight against crime and middle-class flight, many are looking to Five Oaks and other barricaded neighborhoods as a model.

The New Maginot Line: Miami Shores, Florida

The city of Miami Shores resembles a movie set, not a real place to live. It has as a backdrop Biscayne Bay, the same view that framed so many episodes of the "Miami Vice" television show. The streets are lush with palm trees, pines, and eucalyptus. At the bayfront are exclusive mansions, giving way to progressively less expensive rings of homes, but none less than solid middle class. It seems a small town, just two and a half square miles, but it lies on the edge of the big city of Miami, and its streets run seamlessly from the bay into the grid of Miami.

Our guide to Miami Shores was Jay Beach, the city works director, a polished and tanned civic official. He is tough and knowledgeable. He represents himself as a no-nonsense manager who knows his city and his people. He knows that his city is an island in a sprawling metropolitan area and pointed out the beauty of his town and what he perceives as the squalor of the adjoining city of Miami.

The boulevard that marks the border of Miami Shores also marks the end of the pristine movie-set environment. On the other side of the street, in Miami, is a working-class to poor black neighborhood. Some of its houses need paint, and there are cars up on blocks and trash in the streets. The two sides differ not just in race and income but also in the level of services their respective cities can provide. We are told that garbage pickup is so erratic and insufficient in the Miami neighborhood that its residents frequently just walk their trash across the street for collection on the Shores' garbage day.

It is not just plastic bags on trash day that cross the boulevard. According to Jay Beach, crime, disorder, and vandalism also come from the other side. Unchecked, he thinks it would have led to the decline of the Shores, at least in the blocks bordering Miami, and he wholeheartedly supports the solution that the town found: barricading the streets.

It all began in 1988 as a mayoral campaign promise to improve public safety. The candidate, soon elected mayor, also promised an open style of government in which he would obtain citizen input on the most serious problems. The first citywide meeting was attended by an unprecedented several thousand citizens. No one has seen a meeting of that size before or since. Public safety concerns dominated the evening, especially the decay of the Miami neighborhoods across the eastern border. The general perception was that crime in Miami Shores came from the neighborhoods to the east.

There had recently been a series of drive-by purse snatchings, victimizing people in their own driveways. Women said they were petrified to go outside. Old people felt terrorized by roving hoodlums who could penetrate their neighborhoods from any one of several major roadways and flee before any police response was possible. The city was perceived to be too vulnerable. The answer that came out of the meeting was simple: secure the perimeter.

The proposal to install barricades to close off streets along the border was placed in the hands of a citizen task force. They came up with an extreme plan that called for a system of barricades that would seal off virtually all entrances to the city from Miami and create a maze within it using internal barricades. Only the most major thoroughfares would be left open.

The Miami Shores city council reacted to the plan with shock. The plan was too extreme and controversial. They feared it might violate state law on access and create a public safety nightmare for the police and fire departments. The task force report was rejected, but the mayoral promise had to be kept. More citizen input was elicited, and hearings were held on a less drastic plan developed by the city manager. The plan reduced the number of barricades, concentrating those that remained on the eastern border. But even this scaled-back plan divided the city. Members of the mayor's task force felt betrayed. A hard-core group of residents from all over Miami Shores felt any barricading was unconstitutional, antidemocratic, and racially motivated. The city council held its ground. There would be some barricades, but they would be modest and control access, not seal off neighborhoods. Finally a plan was approved, with a few internal barricades to satisfy political pressures. The city manager was given the go-ahead to develop an implementation plan and design the barricades.

The street barricades were designed by Randall Atlas, a local architect and security consultant. They are essentially landscaped beds of shrubs across the streets, which create cul-de-sacs ending in palm trees, foliage, and reflective signs. In places it is difficult to tell that the street pattern was ever any different. But the eastern neighbors considered the barricades a personal affront, no matter how attractive. Initially, opponents drove trucks through the barricades, and the shrubbery was regularly destroyed. City officials fortified them to withstand vehicular intrusions by adding cement curbs, rail ties, and metal posts. The strategy worked. The barricades now stand unmolested.

More requests were made to extend the system to the next level and in essence wall off neighborhoods internally. The city council has steadfastly refused to do this for both policy and pragmatic reasons. Any further barricading might impede transportation routes and incur the wrath of Dade County or the state of Florida. And at least some on the council, though happy to block off Miami Shores from Miami, see blocking off neighborhoods of the Shores from each other as detrimental to community.

Do these barriers work? No one can know for sure. Some forms of crime are down, but the role of the barricades in this is unproved. Whatever the reality, residents report a stronger feeling of security, a greater willingness to walk their own streets. But conflict remains over the specific locations of the barricades and over the barricades themselves. Some early opponents of the plan have even moved away, as have others who failed to get barricades exactly where they wanted them.

The bitterness over the barricades is still part of the political fabric. It is an issue that is almost constantly before the city council. Some Miami Shores neighborhoods feel the barricades diverted traffic and crime toward them. Others feel the barricades are too small and insufficient an answer. No matter where residents stand on this sensitive issue, the topic will not die. Miami Shores is now behind the barricades; the question is, on which side of the gate is the lock?

Crime and Community in the Security Zone

Inner-city and lower-income neighborhoods are desperate, and suburban neighborhoods, watching urban problems creep closer, are worried. The issues that concern the city, suburb, and barricade perches are similar to those that concern the lifestyle and prestige communities: control, privacy, security, fear. The difference in the security zones is that they feel the pressures of traffic, crime, and fear within their neighborhoods or spilling over from nearby, and they take the initiative to try to regain or control their territory by building gates or barricades.

Many security zone neighborhoods have known real community and are fighting to retain or regain it. Community is more than a commodity in these instances; it is a sense of both shared territory and shared destiny. The community residents are not willing to uproot themselves, fleeing farther and farther from the center of the metropolis, but are fighting to retain their neighborhoods and their quality of life. But are gates the answer?

Gates often embroil localities in conflict, both internal and external, as we have seen. Conflict can be even more intense in barricade perches, even though they are not complete closures, because the streets remain public. Racial tensions often emerge when barricading or gating is discussed, as they did in Maplewood and Newark, New Jersey, and in Miami Shores.

In the Coconut Grove area of Miami, the predominantly Caribbean-American west Grove has rallied against installing gates or barricades in the other, wealthier quarters of the Grove, viewing them as part of a racist plot. A local planner told us that some of the affluent Grove residents had said that rather than place barricades in their neighborhoods, the west Grove should be barricaded off, to keep poverty and crime contained.[23]

The U.S. Department of Housing and Urban Development launched an investigation into Houston's numerous street closures in late 1994. The city had adopted an ordinance to allow street closures for traffic control and safety. A group of residents complained that many of the closures were discriminatory and racially motivated, arguing that census data confirm that several neighborhoods have been split along racial lines by street closures.[24] In 1993, when Mayor Richard M. Daley proposed a plan to "cul-de-sac" the city of Chicago with concrete barriers, the outcry was enormous. Still smarting from the erection of street barricades by suburbs trying to block the city out, many Chicagoans felt the barriers would divide the city by race and class, isolating the poor and people of color from the city they felt rightfully belonged to all.

Despite these conflicts, more and more neighborhoods are considering barricades in the attempt to protect their homes, streets, and lives. The scattered local data on the effectiveness of barricading are anecdotal and inconclusive, with examples of less crime, greater crime, and no change at all. Some report lower crime in adjacent areas, some higher. Some neighborhoods have removed gates or barricades in disappointment or frustration after having fought to build them. Others remain barricaded peacefully and successfully, inspiring other neighborhoods to emulate them.

Closed-street neighborhoods in St. Louis were compared with similar open-street neighborhoods in the mid-1970s by Oscar Newman, a planner who consults with governments and neighborhoods to design gating plans. That study found great variations in the incidence of crime, but in general, the open, public streets had more crime than the private, closed streets.[25] The biggest difference between the open- and closed-street neighborhoods was in perception: those behinds gates felt much safer on their streets and were more likely to leave doors and windows open.

Two of the more thorough and wide-ranging studies were conducted by police in Ft. Lauderdale. The first found no significant change in rates for violent or property crime in a closed-street neighborhood. For auto theft, burglary, and some other crimes, there were sometimes considerable drops immediately after closure, but none were sustained for more than a short time.[26] A second study (see table 5-2), conducted in 1990 by the Ft. Lauderdale Police Crime Prevention Unit, compared the change in crime rates in several closed-street neighborhoods with that of the city as a whole and concluded that the gates and barricades had no significant effect. A simultaneous survey of patrol officers found that the majority dislike the street closures; most think that they do not reduce crime but do slow emergency response time and inhibit police patrols.[27]

The theory behind the street closures, crime prevention through environmental design (CPTED), holds that anything that increases a neighborhood's sense of territoriality or pride of place will help reduce crime. The major thrust is the creation of "defensible space," or clear physical boundaries that residents will be willing and able to watch and defend. Whatever physical design changes are made, a key element of a successful CPTED effort is the strengthening of community cohesion and involvement. However, the Ft. Lauderdale officers report that they have witnessed conflict and division in several neighborhoods as residents fight over the planning and approval of barricades. Noting the importance of resident cooperation, they warn that street closure plans have polarized some neighborhoods and shattered existing organizations. Certainly this was the outcome in Whitley Heights.

With white and middle-class flight from many central cities accel-

Table 5-2. *Crime Rate Trends in Ft. Lauderdale Neighborhoods, 1988–89*

	Change from previous years (%)	
Type of neighborhood	1988	1989
Barricaded neighborhoods[a]		
Riverside Park	−18	6
Sunrise Intracoastal	−6	−2
Tarpon River	−3	−8
Edgewood		−8
Average	−7	−3
Open neighborhoods[b]		
Coral Ridge	−15	0
Dorsey Riverbend	−18	6
Ft. Lauderdale Beach	−9	−5
River Oaks	6	−9
Victoria Park	−13	9
Riverland	−7	−2
So. Middle River	−18	−2
Croissant Park	−10	−6
Poinsetta Heights	−2	−6
North East Progresso	−11	−18
Melrose Manors	−9	14
Shady Banks	−13	15
Lauderdale Manors	−1	−11
North East Ft. Lauderdale	−9	−2
Coral Ridge Isles	−8	-4
Average	−9	−1
Citywide average	−11	−2

Source: Crime Prevention and Research Units, *Street Closure Study* (Ft. Lauderdale, Fla.: Ft. Lauderdale Police Department, 1990).

a. Barricaded neighborhoods include all those whose boundaries coincide with police reporting areas and which had street barricades installed during the full year.

b. Open neighborhoods include all whose boundaries coincide with police reporting areas.

erating, community is the only way that inner cities will be preserved. The barricades create islands of security that may change perceptions, but they will hardly help stem the tide of departures. Many of the Miami neighborhoods we visited were on the brink. In Coconut Grove a resident fighting to close the streets of his neighborhood claimed that "barricading is logical, because the quality of life is terrible here."[28]

The security zone represents a fight for territorial control of neighborhood, but it is a fight with many motivations. Some of the street closures of the perches are based on convenience, a simple desire to reduce traffic. Others are based on a desire for prestige or exclusivity, or on a desire to increase property values or protect gentrified space. Many others are expressions of real problems. Efforts by privileged or gentrified neighborhoods to insulate themselves from those poorer than themselves are questionable bases for community in a democratic society. But at the same time, efforts to protect and defend neighborhoods experiencing real threats cannot be denigrated. They represent a communal effort at problem solving. Even if the solution is of questionable effectiveness, community organization and initiative toward improving neighborhoods is a positive step.

6

You Can Run, But You Can't Hide

SOME PEOPLE are drawn to gates for prestige, image, and status. Some are looking for privacy. Some want to privatize by buying and controlling their own common space and services. Some want a country club, an exclusive place to enjoy their favorite forms of recreation. Some want to protect themselves from crime and traffic. All want control—over their homes, their streets, their neighborhoods. Through gates, guards, and walls they seek this control in the ability to exclude outsiders from their territory. In this chapter we look at the results of our national survey of gated communities to further examine the motivations and experiences of the residents of gated communities.

Behind the Gates: Safety

Security and fear of crime is one of the most important issues in the nation. Almost 90 percent of Americans think crime is getting worse; 55 percent worry about becoming a victim of crime, and the same percent-

Figure 6-1. *The Importance of Security in the Choice of a Gated Community*

Percentage of respondents

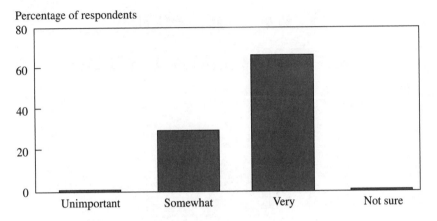

Source: Authors' survey, 1995.

age feel inadequately protected by the police.[1] The results of our survey of homeowner association boards show that security is likewise a primary concern for those who buy in gated communities. The respondents thought that they and their neighbors were drawn to fortifications around their subdivisions; nearly 70 percent indicated that security was a very important issue in their decision to live in their gated communities. Security was not an important motivation for only 1 percent (see figure 6-1).

The gated communities in this study are thus part of the dramatic growth of the security industry. A 1993 National Institute of Justice study reported that three times as many people work in the security field, from equipment manufacturers to armored-car drivers, as are employed by official law-enforcement agencies. In the decade from the early 1980s to the early 1990s, the number of security guards doubled and surpassed the number of police. Private security outspends public law enforcement by 73 percent and is the nation's primary protective resource.[2]

Residents told us repeatedly that they want to protect themselves from crime, reduce traffic, and control their neighborhoods. And they believe that the gates work. More than two-thirds of the respondents believed there was less crime in their developments than in the surround-

Figure 6-2. *Perception of Gate as a Factor in Crime Reduction*

Percentage of respondents

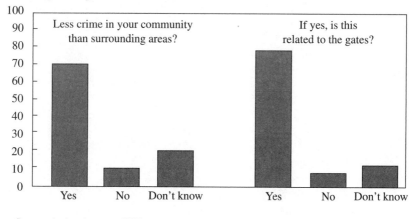

Source: Authors' survey, 1995.

ing areas. Of those, a full 80 percent attributed the difference to the gates (see figure 6-2).

Many nongated communities also have some type of security. The general survey of homeowner associations conducted by the Community Associations Institute, of which our survey of gated communities was a part, found that in addition to the 19 percent of developments that are gated, another 27 percent have some other form of security such as a perimeter wall or a roving patrol. Only 54 percent have no security of any type, even a perimeter fence. The survey asked respondents whether they felt that the level of crime in their development was lower than, higher than, or equal to the level in the surrounding area, and the results were analyzed by the type of security they reported having (see figure 6-3). Not surprisingly, the higher the level of security, the safer respondents were likely to feel. Although 41 percent of the respondents from developments with no security reported that they had less crime than their surrounding areas, those with some type of security were all much more likely to report lower levels of crime. Interestingly, only a tiny percentage in each case, no matter what type of security was used, reported that crime was higher in their developments. The highest percentages believing that they had less crime lived in developments with

Figure 6-3. *Perceived Level of Crime, by Type of Security*

Percentage of respondents

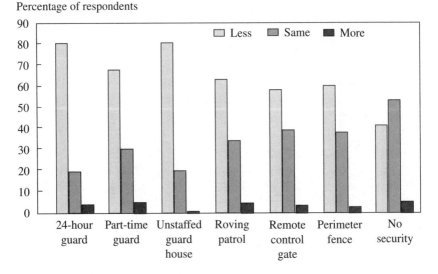

Source: Doreen Heisler and Warren Klein, *Inside Look at Community Association Home-ownership: Facts and Perceptions* (Alexandria, Va.: Community Associations Institute, 1996), p. 16.

unstaffed guardhouses or twenty-four-hour guards, at 81 and 80 percent) respectively. Sixty-seven percent of those with a part-time guard reported a lower level of crime, and 58 percent of those with a remote control gate reported a lower level of crime. About half of the respondents with no security reported that they had the same level of crime as the surrounding area; in all other categories a much lower percentage did so.

Is this perception of greater safety behind gates supported by evidence? The ambiguous and spotty successes and failures of gates and barricades as crime control measures, discussed in chapter 5, indicate that although people may feel safer, they probably are not significantly safer.

Fear and anxiety feed on themselves. Gates and walls reflect fear and serve as daily reminders of the perceived dangers on the other side, and at the same time they do little to improve the reality. Even if crime is lower in the gated communities, the city and suburban streets outside are unchanged. But of course there is more than the fear of crime behind the wave of gating. Gates are reassuring in the face of anxiety levels heightened by economic, demographic, and social change. They shield us from a world where we feel vulnerable.

Some proponents of gated communities argue that by providing private security, these developments are relieving the public policing burden, freeing resources to be used elsewhere. In most cases, however, private security measures augment rather than replace police services. This is especially true where residential street patrols are not a significant part of police activities, as in the low-crime suburbs where gated communities are most common. Yet the result is not more publicly provided security for those outside gated areas, but rather a two-tiered system of security: more for those who pay to supplement police with private security, and less for those who cannot or do not do so. Frank Turner, the director of the Development Services Department for the city of Plano, Texas, contends, "If we are going to argue that this is necessary for safety and security, then we ought to require them for all new developments. Why should you say anyone should have second-rate security?"[3]

Behind the Gates: Community

There are reasons to expect that putting up walls and fences and gating the entrance to a development will strengthen the area as a community. Proponents of gated communities often argue that by allowing neighborhoods to establish and protect their boundaries and to control access to their territory, the residents of gated communities will develop a sense of identity and security, both of which are vital to strong communities. At least for place-based community, the importance of boundaries, of knowing what is "ours" and what is outside, is a theme in much of the literature on community.[4] Known physical borders can help govern social interaction, reduce conflict, and stimulate the feelings of territoriality and ownership that bond people together and create grounds for interdependence and mutual action.

Other characteristics of gated communities, which they share with all private homeowner associations, also have been seen by many as encouraging not only a sense of community but also community action.[5] These include homogeneity in income, interests, and lifestyle, resulting from the micro-division of developments into separate subdivisions according to housing type; the existence of a structure for self-government, for communication, and for institutional cohesion in the form of the homeowner association; and a degree of economic interdependence resulting from shared ownership of common areas and facilities, streets, and, in the case of attached dwellings, even roofs and walls.

The concept of community in this book refers to both the community of sentiment—the "good feelings" and sense of belonging that most Americans are referring to when they speak of community—and to the community of public participation and involvement toward mutual ends. Studies of community satisfaction, a related concept, should not be confused with community feeling or community ties. Satisfaction is not participation, just as an identification with a place is not the same as a feeling of belonging. Satisfaction and identification are one-way connections to a place or a group, while participation and belonging represent real connection, the two-way involvement that community, as we have defined it, demands.

Our survey was designed to gauge how the residents of gated communities feel about their developments and how much they participate in their neighborhood social life and governance. One pair of survey questions asked about the degree of community feeling perceived by the respondents and how they thought it compared with community feeling in other nearby developments. Most respondents report that their developments are "friendly," but only 8 percent said they were "neighborly and tight-knit." A surprising 28 percent were willing to say their neighborhoods were "distant or private" in feeling. And although more than a third think that the level of community feeling within their developments is better than in most developments around them, the plurality report that it is "about the same" as elsewhere (see figure 6-4).

The CAI survey added a question on community feeling almost identical to ours for gated communities, which was answered by all respondents in the sample (see figure 6-5). To isolate the effect of gates as much as possible, we compared the responses from gated communities with those from the entire sample of private developments with homeowner associations.[6] The respondents from gated communities were somewhat more likely to describe the level of community feeling in their developments as "friendly" than was the sample as a whole. Fifty-eight percent of all those surveyed and 68 percent of those in gated communities felt their developments were friendly. The same proportion of the entire sample and of the respondents from gated communities,

Figure 6-4. *Perceived Level of Community in Gated Communities Compared with Surrounding Areas*

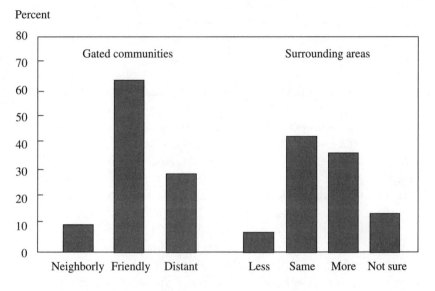

Percent

Source: Heisler and Klein, *Inside Look*.

Figure 6-5. *Perceptions of Community Feeling*

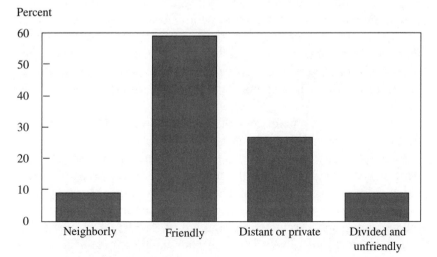

Percent

Source: Heisler and Klein, *Inside Look*.

8 percent, described their developments as "neighborly and tight-knit." Approximately one-third of all respondents and one-quarter of gated community respondents reported lesser levels of community feeling.

These findings are in keeping with other work on the reported level of community feeling. In a random survey of residents of Orange County, California, Mark Baldassare and Georjeanna Wilson found that 68 percent felt they lived in places with a sense of community.[7] The survey included those in both urban and suburban areas of predominantly suburban Orange County. They found that those in areas with "urban" characteristics—higher percentages of minorities, higher density, and larger city size—were less likely to report a sense of community. Other factors that correlated significantly with a sense of community were the respondents' satisfaction with the amount of privacy from their neighbors and their satisfaction with the amount of general participation they perceived to be occurring around city or neighborhood issues.

The survey results also accord with the qualitative data gathered through a dozen focus groups in gated communities. We found high levels of residential satisfaction almost everywhere we went; people were proud of their neighborhoods and generally saw them as friendly places. The survey results indicate that although most gated community residents do not feel their developments have any greater level of community feeling than developments in the surrounding area, a significant 33 percent do think they are more neighborly. And when the responses from gated communities are compared with those from the sample as a whole, a somewhat higher percentage see their developments as having at least moderate levels of community feeling. As some of the residents we interviewed told us, gates may help residents identify with their neighborhoods, recognize their neighbors, and feel more safe and open in social interaction.

But is this effect merely one of comfort, however important it may be to residential satisfaction and quality of life? Or does it extend to participation in community life, to feelings of shared interest and interdependence—the public face of community? To examine this issue of community as participation, our survey asked questions about the level of involvement in the homeowner association, both as a mini-government and as a social vehicle (see figure 6-6). The board members surveyed reported much lower levels of community involvement than of community feeling. Only 6 percent reported that residents were "very

Figure 6-6. *Level of Involvement*

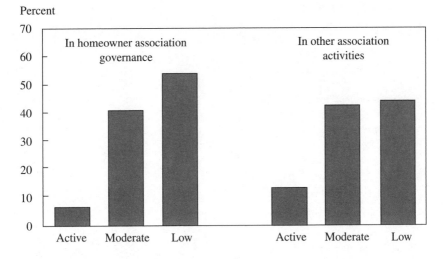

Source: Authors' survey, 1995.

active" in governance; a majority of respondents, 55 percent, said residents were not active. Levels of participation in social activities were higher than in governance. Thirteen percent reported that residents were "very active" in nongovernance association activities like block parties and newcomer welcoming. The remainder were nearly evenly divided between "somewhat" and "not" active, at 41 and 46 percent, respectively.

The main body of the CAI survey, directed at both gated and nongated communities, did not ask the same question, so direct comparisons are impossible. However, the survey did ask respondents to indicate and rank factors contributing to development problems. One of these factors was "apathy/lack of interest," which also measures levels of participation and involvement in association governance. Approximately the same proportion of gated and nongated communities reported that apathy was the most significant factor leading to problems in their developments (21 percent of gated communities and 22 percent of nongated). For both gated and nongated communities, apathy was the second most frequently cited cause of problems, running behind residents' not understanding the rules (see figure 6-7). A related factor was "lack of opportunity for participation," which 3 percent of respondents from gated communities

Figure 6-7. *Factors Contributing to Problems: Gated versus Nongated Communities*[a]

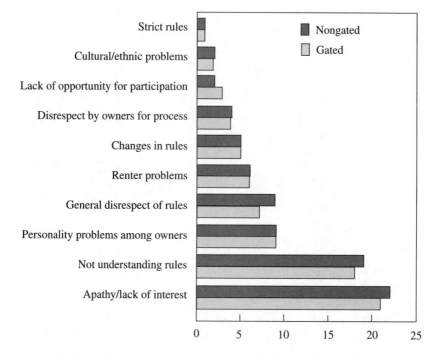

Source: Heisler and Klein, *Inside Look.*

a. Other factors given as choices, all indicated by less than 10 percent of respondents, related to HOA boards and management.

and 2 percent of those from nongated communities cited. Similarly, 4 percent of respondents in both categories indicated that "disrespect by owners for process" was a source of problems.

The degree of apathy and of other involvement-related concerns that respondents reported in both gated and nongated communities was essentially the same, even as gated communities reported somewhat higher levels of community feeling. These responses would seem to confirm our analysis that although gates may help residents identify with their developments, recognize their neighbors, and feel more social, they do not in and of themselves produce any stronger ties or feelings of interdependence.

As we discussed in chapter 2, studies have found little evidence that homeowner associations breed higher levels of participation and self-governance. Some argue that this is due to free-rider problems or flawed structures or processes, others that it is due to basing public roles on private property ownership, or to a general lack of participatory consciousness in society.[8] Whatever the reason, it is clear that gates do not help to increase participation or overcome apathy. Both problems exist in gated communities as well as in nongated communities and in society at large.

Because gated communities have clear boundaries and the advantage of organized communications through built-in homeowner associations, clubs, and other vehicles designed to include members in the social structure, one might expect more community spirit or closeness in gated developments. But this seems not to be the case. Although their structure might well support strong community feeling, it does not create it. Neighborhood in the sense of a collectively identified boundary can be physically created, but neighborhood in the sense of mutual responsibility is much harder to produce. Gated communities are no better or worse than society as a whole in producing a strong sense of collective citizenship. At least theoretically, they offer a better platform for mutual interaction and cooperative spirit than more open settlements, and yet we have seen no indication that they are any more successful at achieving them.

The Limits of Separate Space

It is no accident that developers refer to their products as "communities," and some gated developments, especially lifestyle developments, go to great lengths to create a sense of community for their residents. Desert Horizons, near Palm Springs, California, has its own newsletter, *Horizons*, "Published for the Fortunate Four Hundred." It features photos of residents at association events such as holiday and newcomer welcoming parties and columns offering golf tips, tournament results, and a calendar of events.

Such efforts at stimulating community do not seem to create more neighborly environments or to spawn more community involvement than exist in similar nongated developments. Briarwood and Carlton Square, two gated communities of about 3,000 people in Inglewood, California, are examples. Despite the fact that residents have held public office and voting rates are high, both have a reputation for taking little part in the life of the city. Inside the gates it seems that involvement is also lacking. The president of Carlton Square's homeowner association reports poor attendance at monthly meetings. And a twenty-year resident of Briarwood says the development is "very, very private. You really don't know your neighbors, that's the lifestyle here."[9]

"Common-interest communities" is a term frequently used for homeowner associations. The phrase might seem odd in light of the data; interests in common seem to be limited to financial responsibility for common areas and amenities and a concern for property values. However, the term does speak to the positive side of localism and associational government, a case that has been made most recently by communitarian thinkers like Amitai Etzioni.[10] Increased solidarity and strengthened bonds between neighbors seem patently positive; in fact, they are the base for all participation in public life. Certainly the residents of walled cities see their security systems as enabling neighborliness and community. The reason that residents can feel their gated neighborhoods to be stronger communities than others and yet evince no sign of greater involvement in those communities is the difference between the two facets of community: the private side of sentiment and the public side of participation. The ties behind the gates are formed for individual, private ends—protection of property and the quality of life of the household. In this our results differ little from the findings of some other researchers on suburbanites and community. David Hummon found that suburban residents see their towns and neighborhoods not as communities of common ties and shared social interaction but as the locus for private life—clean, quiet, safe, secure places of retreat for domicile and family.[11]

Another side to the question of community is, How connected to the larger community are the residents of gated developments? Do they view themselves, their lives, and their future as tied up with the cities and regions outside their gates? Community within a neighborhood is important but is not sufficient to promote the health of a neighborhood or a nation. Community must extend beyond the neighborhood to the broader community of which the residential area is just one part.

The question of whether it is possible to sustain a healthy public or private life without commitment to the larger community, of the balance between individualism and community, is an old one in America. As Tocqueville defined it, "Individualism is a calm and considered feeling which disposes each citizen to isolate himself from the mass of his fellows and withdraw into a circle of family and friends; with this little society formed to his taste, he gladly leaves the greater society to look after itself."[12]

In his study of individualism and community in American life, Robert Bellah found that although the balance has not shifted completely to the side of individualism in America, many have chosen to surround themselves with similar people in suburban tracts, satisfied with a narrow definition of community that extends only to those in their lifestyle enclaves. Our interviews, data, and experience in gated communities strongly reflect the picture drawn by Bellah and his colleagues. In fact, they found one suburbanite who has by now likely moved into a gated community. Talking about his growing suburb, he told the researchers: "I wish we could have bought twenty acres back then [1959]—twenty acres in the back country—and put a moat around it with alligators in it. A good community is when you have a complete mixture—enough shopping to take care of your needs, but not large shopping centers that would bring people in from outside the community. I would want to see our community develop as if it were an island."[13]

Gated communities have created a new housing option for some of us, but they have also created a new societal dilemma for all of us. The purpose of gates and walls is to limit social contact, and reduced social contact may weaken the ties that form the social contract. As one realtor in a focus group in California said, "It is a form of elitism—so they don't have to fraternize with folks from the city center."[14] Another observed that some residents, who had come from Oakland or Los Angeles, for instance, were sensitive to greater societal problems, if not to the same degree as before their move to the suburban gated community. A number of those present agreed with her. One maintained that those who had never lived in a city or other area of mixed incomes and experienced the problems faced by other classes would not care at all.

Others who have researched gated enclaves have found a similar narrowing of connections. When Oscar Newman compared the closed streets of St. Louis with their nongated counterparts, he found that residents of the closed, private streets were more likely to define their neighborhood as their gated street. Among the residents of the open, public streets, only a few limited the definition of their neighborhood to the street on which they lived.[15]

In an open city, even if somewhat segregated, people of different colors and incomes must negotiate their mutual fate together. In some respects, they learn to value one another more highly, and social networks are expanded. In socially isolated environments, social distance leads to stereotyping and misunderstanding, which in turn leads to fear and even greater distance. A resident in one of our focus groups exemplified this dynamic when she told us that she never left her downtown San Francisco office building, even for lunch, for fear of the people on the streets. Her building is located on a central street of department stores and offices, populated at lunch hour mainly by businesspeople and shoppers. But because it is a public space where anyone may go, it is too uncontrolled for her comfort, too unpredictable. Unlike her gated suburb, its openness increases the vulnerability she already feels to an unacceptable level.

Our research has examined the stress and contradictions in the ideal of community represented by the gated community form. Residents of gated communities, like other people in cities and suburbs across the country, vary in the degree to which they personally feel the connections and duties of community within and outside their developments. The difference is that in gated communities, with their privatized streets, recreation, local governance, and security, residents have less need of the public realm outside their gates than those living in traditional open neighborhoods. If they choose to withdraw, there are fewer ties to break, less daily dependence on the greater community.

Similar issues are brought up by homeowner associations in general. The question is of the level of autonomy of these microgovernments, of the degree to which they and their residents can act independently of and apart from larger jurisdictions. Most homeowner associations, for example, ban house-to-house canvassing and all signs other than "for sale" signs. This means that candidates for public office and party workers cannot call on residents to get out the vote and supporters cannot post political signs. With gates, excluding that part of the democratic process is even more easily enforced. To Greg Alexander, the problem of exclusion is the core dilemma of community:

There is a constant risk that groups may develop into nomic bunkers. The experience of group life will exacerbate, rather than resolve, the problem of alienation if groups themselves exist as autonomous units, unconnected with others. To realize their potential for creating community, groups must be held to an obligation more demanding than mere compliance with their own internal aspirations. Groups must accept a civic obligation to maintain community within our society. Meeting that obligation requires a praxis of openness and dialogue. . . . [This dialogue] can occur even while boundaries are maintained; indeed it may require boundaries. But it cannot occur in the presence of walls.[16]

Alexander is referring to legal walls rather than physical ones, but his point applies to both types of barriers.

Not all gated community residents feel that they are fully in charge of their own destinies, despite their seeming control over their infrastructure and territory. In Cottonwood Valley, for example, even the childless participants in our focus group were knowledgeable and concerned about their predominately minority school district in Irving, Texas, because they saw the links between themselves and their surrounding environment. In Marblehead, Canyon Lake, and other gated communities, the obvious porosity of their fenced borders has forced residents to acknowledge the futility of pretending they are a land apart.

But these were exceptions in our visits to gated communities across the nation. Most residents believed they had successfully placed themselves beyond the range of troubles in the outside world.

The trend toward privatized government and neighborhoods is part of the more general trend of fragmentation, and the resulting loss of connection and social contact is narrowing the bonds of mutual responsibility and the social contract. Almost imperceptibly, the societal idea of what it means to be a resident of a community seems to have changed; it is more common now to speak of taxpayers than of citizens.

Taxpayers pay tribute to the government, and they receive services from it. So does every subject of a totalitarian regime. What taxpayers do not do, and what people who call themselves taxpayers have long since stopped even imagining doing, is governing. In a democracy, by the very meaning of the word, when the people govern they create among themselves the conditions for their lives and mutual reinforcing associations.[17]

In gated communities and other privatized enclaves, the local community that many residents identify with is the one within the gates. Their homeowner association dues are like taxes; and their responsibility to their community, such as it is, ends at that gate. Even if this withdrawal from the public realm is not unique to gated communities but endemic in society as a whole, gates and fences manifest this withdrawal in a strong physical symbol of exclusion that sends a message to all outside. One city official in Plano, Texas, summed up his view of the attitude of the gated community residents in his town: "'I took care of my responsibility, I'm safe in here, I've got my guard gate; I've paid my [homeowner association] dues, and I'm responsible for my streets. Therefore, I have no responsibility for the commonweal, because you take care of your own.'"[18]

The State of Gates

Embarking on a research project like this is much like entering a gated community for the first time—one has some preconceptions, but the reality is in many ways surprising. First, inside the gates, it was surprising how similar these developments were to other contemporary housing tracts. Their residents, too, were not really different from their counterparts in nongated communities, in part because few set out to live in a gated community—another surprise. Most of the people we spoke to chose their housing and its location primarily for other factors, and for some their residence in a gated community was almost accidental. Even so, as reflected in the survey results, for a large majority the gates had become an important and welcome feature.

We were also surprised by how porous the defenses really were, how easy they were to breach. We were intimidated at first by the gates, guards, and the process of asking permission to enter and confirming our identities when expected by a resident. Quickly, however, as we got used to the pattern, we realized that ease of entry was largely tied to guards' perceptions: a tie, a suit, and a nice car were often enough to be waved past. At unguarded gates, we learned that it was simple to "tailgate" in after the car before us. In one development with a remote-control gate, a resident in the exit lane even stopped to tell us the entry code, politely sparing us the trouble of calling in to our hosts for admission.

Security mechanisms have become so ubiquitous in America, from office buildings to airports, that we have become desensitized to them. Even as we become more impatient, less respectful, and more adept at avoiding their inconveniences, we are turning to them with increasing frequency, demanding more guards, more fences, more protection.

We have asked how people think about gated communities, and what opinions residents, planners, developers, and city governments have of them. For the most part, they are taken for granted. Public debate is not yet common, except in street closure cases. Gated communities in southern California and elsewhere are now part of the cultural landscape. The planning profession in general is only just beginning to address the issues surrounding gated communities. Most residents view gates simply as one of many amenities chosen to fit and reflect their lifestyle and to protect their property values. In choosing a house and a subdivision, for most the gates were a secondary, but positive, consideration. Most said that they had never really thought about the gates guarding their neighborhoods; yet everyone we interviewed, even those who had mixed feelings about their gates, said that if asked they would vote to keep them.

We also looked at the experiences and attitudes of the residents of the gated communities, the degree of community existing in these places, and the extent to which their boundaries and identities define them. Our survey respondents from gated communities indicated slightly higher levels of positive community feeling than did the respondents from all homeowner associations. Certainly the physical boundaries that define gated communities seem to contribute to a stronger sense of identification with the place, if not necessarily with the people residing there. In some places we visited, the greater perception of safety behind gates made some feel freer to walk about and socialize in their neighborhoods, but others reported no such effect. In our site visits and focus group interviews, we found that most social interaction, visits with neighbors, and mutual support activities took place, not surprisingly, among those who shared recreation interests or the same street or cul-de-sac.

We also addressed the practice of citizenship among residents of gated communities—the degree to which they perceived themselves to be part of a larger community and their level of connection or involvement outside the gates. We found little evidence of outright hostility to the outside world. In at least some cases, gates serve as physical manifestations of psychological and social distance from other communities and citizens. But in general, those inside the gated communities think little about the ramifications of their housing choice for others outside. Some, although far from all, are in retreat and loath to share their resources with other citizens. Others care deeply about the local school system, and others volunteer with local charities. We also found residents who feared and avoided the towns and regions where they lived, preferring to stay inside their walls. Gated community residents may not be significantly more withdrawn than others in their immediate area or even in the country as a whole, but they have the hardware that allows them to achieve the desired degree of distance. Residents of open neighborhoods do not.

We have looked at many different kinds of gated communities and the reasons people build gates and choose to live behind them. Some are protecting themselves from crime on their very doorsteps, others are fearful that crime may one day reach their streets. Some want prestige, an image, status. Some are looking for privacy. Some want to privatize, buying and controlling their own common space and services. Some want a country club, an exclusive place to enjoy their favorite forms of recreation. Some are trying to find community and hope that a gate and a wall will help define it and bring the people inside together. All want control over their homes, their streets, their neighborhoods. All want to feel less vulnerable.

But what does this mean for the country as a whole, for our cities, our regions, and our neighborhoods? Where will the gating trend lead? One way to begin to see what the gating of America might mean is to look at those places where gates have become more common, where they are the norm rather than the exception.

On the coast of South Carolina, Hilton Head Island is a honeycomb of gated communities, with so many walls surrounding private developments that there is no possible route for a badly needed new cross-island road. In the contiguous towns of the Coachella Valley in California, where Palm Springs is located, gates and walls are everywhere. Along Highway 123, the four-lane main road through the valley, walls line both sides of the street, broken only by vacant land and the commercial strips.

In areas of Orange County, California, where gated communities have been built in large numbers since the 1980s, walls and fences line the roads, and gates are ubiquitous. The effect is startling to the driver who is unaccustomed to the sight. The roads through residential areas feel almost like freeways, complete with sound walls. There are more exits than on a freeway, to be sure, but they are only for those who have a pass to get by the guard or a code to open the gate.

The residents of gated communities seek security, but more broadly they seek control. They want to control crime and traffic. They want to be free from strangers, disruptions, intrusions. They want privacy, stability, peace of mind, familiarity. They want to protect their economic status and their investment in their home. All of these motivations are understandable and valid. But the questions that gated communities raise go beyond their benefits for the people who live inside them. In the next chapter, we look at the larger social issues that underlie and are reflected in the proliferation of gated communities.

7

Not-So-Brave
New World

AMERICA IS increasingly divided by income, race, and economic opportunity. There can be little doubt that the resulting urban problems are part of the stimulus for the wave of gating. The drive for separation, distinction, exclusion, and protection has also been fueled by the dramatic demographic and social changes of the second half of the twentieth century. The original suburban movement was based in nostalgia for peaceful small-town life and separation from the problems of industrialization. In the middle of the century, suburbs expanded with the affluence of a new middle class and their flight from the poor and minorities living in the inner cities.

Today, with that nostalgia as strong as ever and a new set of problems pressing on our metropolitan areas, separation is still the solution that Americans turn to. In the suburbs, gates are the logical extension of the original suburban drive. In the city, gates and barricades are sometimes called "cul-de-sac-ization"—a term that reflects the design goal to create out of the existing urban grid a street pattern as close to suburban patterns as possible. Gates are an attempt to suburbanize our cities and intensify the patterns of our suburbs.

Gated communities are a symbol of the underlying tensions in the social fabric. When combined with patterns of racial and economic segregation, income polarization, and exclusionary land use practices, the symbolic impact of gated communities is even more acute. Our housing choices are far more complex than simple economic options. They symbolize what we want for our families and communities and what we don't want, what we value and what we fear. This chapter examines the larger trends and issues—race, poverty, crime, fear, and suburbanization—that are the backdrop for the rise of gated communities and then looks at the public debate that gating has prompted.

Separate Settlement: Division and Fragmentation

Separate spaces in our nation are bounded by race and income. Race is not the propelling or only factor, but the coincidence of race, income, and location in America cannot be ignored.[1] There is no question that America is a very different place than it was during the 1940s and 1950s, when the suburbs blossomed to house the growing middle class. The nation is more diverse, with larger populations of minorities and high levels of immigration from third world countries. At the beginning of the century there were 76 million U.S. citizens, 88 percent of whom were white. By 1950 the population had doubled to 151 million, with almost the same percentage of whites. However, in 1995, with a population of 263 million, the white population had fallen to 74 percent. The age structure had also changed, with only 4 percent sixty-five years old or older in 1900, and 13 percent in that age group at the end of the twentieth century. By the middle of the next century, forecasts say, the national population may reach 383 million, with the proportion of whites falling to a bare majority of 53 percent and the elderly climbing to 20 percent.[2]

Similar demographic trends are seen in the metropolitan areas with the largest numbers of gated communities. High levels of foreign immigration and a growing underclass are rapidly changing the face of metropolitan areas like Los Angeles, Miami, Chicago, and New York. Along with these demographic changes, there is growing poverty and significant dislocation caused by a restructuring economy. Suburbanization has transformed our metropolitan regions, with center cities losing their place as the center of culture and business. But the suburbs are also changing. In metropolitan areas, poverty and economic inequality are no longer limited to the inner cities. As a map of Los Angeles (figure 7-1) clearly depicts, flight to the suburbs has not meant avoiding all the aspects of poverty associated with the urban core.

The Los Angeles area is the new archetype of metropolitan spatial segregation, in which poverty is no longer concentrated in the central city but is suburbanizing, racing farther and farther out from the metropolitan center. The demand for gates and walls is created and encouraged by these new social changes. Even formerly well established, "good" suburbs now have their share of social and physical structural problems. The suburbs are becoming urbanized, such that many might now be called "outer cities," [3] places with many of the problems and pathologies traditionally thought to be restricted to big cities. Especially in the aging inner-ring suburbs, the concern is no longer with the spillover of city troubles but with the same troubles arising right at home.

In addition to fighting home-grown crime, suburban counties and cities are struggling to maintain their aging infrastructure, to meet the growing demand for social services, and to maintain high standards in their schools. The "downtowns" of the edge cities are confronting congestion, crime, and vacancies, just like their central-city counterparts.[4] Complaints about public services are no longer confined to large cities. As a result, the flight from the cities has been joined by the flight from the near-in suburbs. For many years, the shape of many metropolitan areas has more and more resembled a donut: the declining quality of life and declining population have left a hole in the center city. And as the inner-ring suburbs now also confront urban problems, the flight away from the center is causing the hole to expand.

The dramatic divisions by race and income in U.S. metropolitan areas affect all races—rich, middle class, and poor. As Anthony Downs has said, discussing economic segregation, "conflicts between the nonpoor and the poor interfere with the forging of a strong sense of solidarity between them, particularly because they tend to live in different neighborhoods." Lack of understanding and cooperation between the poor and the nonpoor, he argues, is causing "mutual losses from

Figure 7-1. *The Spatial Patterns of Economic Inequality*

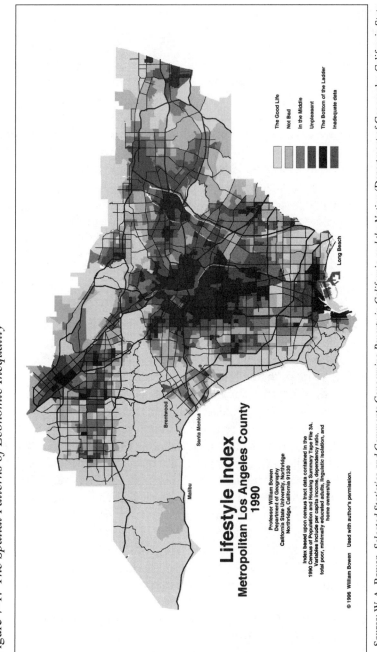

Lifestyle Index
Metropolitan Los Angeles County
1990

Professor William Bowen
Department of Geography
California State University, Northridge
Northridge, California 91330

Index based upon census tract data contained in the
1990 Census of Population and Housing Summary Tape File 3A.
Variables include per capita income, dependency ratio,
total poor, minimally educated adults, linguistic isolation, and
home ownership

© 1996 William Bowen   Used with author's permission.

The Good Life
Not Bad
In the Middle
Unpleasant
The Bottom of the Ladder
Inadequate data

Malibu
Brentwood
Santa Monica
Long Beach

Source: W. A. Bowen, *Selected Statistics and Comments Concerning Poverty in California and the Nation* (Department of Geography, California State University, Northridge, 1994).

the resulting weakening of the overall metropolitan and national economies."[5]

Separation as Segregation

Exclusionary zoning, restrictive covenants, and other means both old and new have been used to separate citizens by race and by class. Similarly, gates and walls are intended to create and maintain quality of life and stability in property values through separation. Anyone who can pay the asking price can move into a gated community, and gates can be had in nearly all price ranges. But those who choose to live behind gates, fences, and barriers do share similar motivations: protection through separation. Gated communities are in part a response to the problems of poverty and crime that are inextricably linked with race in American cities.

White flight is not a thing of the past. Even today, racial mixing in neighborhoods is seen very differently by whites and blacks. Research by Reynolds Farley indicates that while blacks prefer well-integrated neighborhoods in which blacks compose up to half of the residential population, most whites will tolerate only a much smaller black presence.[6] Blacks more than whites hold to the notion of integration as an important social goal because they recognize that both economic and social benefits flow to white areas, white schools, and white work places.

White-black proximity remains a source of underlying social tension, and there has been next to no reduction in racial segregation in the suburbs despite the dramatic increase in minority suburbanization.[7] The number of African Americans living in suburbia grew faster during the 1980s than did the number living in the central-city urban cores. But despite the dramatic increase in minority suburbanization, segregation patterns retain their hold: the majority of people of color living in the suburbs is concentrated in the inner ring and old manufacturing suburbs.[8] In Chicago, for example, as in many metropolitan areas, the inner-ring suburbs are attracting increasing numbers of minorities and immigrants. During the 1980s, nearly as many whites moved out of inner-suburban Cook County as moved out of the city of Chicago, while African Americans and Hispanics moved into both.[9]

Exclusion and racial segregation remain disturbing. Overall rates of racial segregation can be measured by a dissimilarity index, or the percentage of blacks and whites who would have to switch neighborhoods to even the racial distribution throughout a city or metropolitan area. These rates are somewhat lower than in the past, although they remain unacceptably high. In the thirty metropolitan areas with the largest black populations, segregation as measured by dissimilarity was 80.9 in 1970, 75.4, in 1980 and 73.3 in 1990.[10]

Segregation does not diminish with higher income; in the same thirty metropolitan areas, African Americans with incomes of $50,000 or more had a dissimilarity index of 79 on average.[11] Nancy Denton points out that many U.S. metropolitan areas remain not merely segregated but hypersegregated. By this she means that blacks are segregated in four of the five dimensions measured through statistical analysis: dissimilarity (unevenness), isolation, clustering, concentration, and centralization: "The only possible conclusion from these data is that hypersegregation persists and is worsening in nearly all metropolitan areas that were hypersegregated in 1980. . . . Whatever we are doing to combat residential segregation is not nearly enough and in many cases is not working at all."[12]

Segregation is usually thought of in terms of race, but of course it is also economic. National and metropolitan rates of segregation are substantially lower for the poor than for blacks, but where racial segregation has seen some decline since 1970, economic segregation has been increasing (see table 7-1). Segregation of whatever kind has a variety of negative impacts. Geographic, social, and economic isolation lead to reduced opportunity, the concentration of deprivation, and greater vulnerability to economic downturns. Separation and isolation are not just from other members of society, but often also from jobs, adequate public services, and good schools. Douglas Massey, Nancy Denton, and others have argued that racial segregation, by creating and maintaining these neighborhood effects, is the primary factor accounting for the black underclass.[13] Similarly, George Galster, Alan Abramson, and others have pointed out that racially and economically segregated residential patterns are responsible for a "geography of opportunity" that severely disadvantages both minorities and the poor.[14] Claude Fischer and his colleagues argue that a wide range of national policies, including those that have increased residential segregation, set the "rules of the game" that shape individual chances for economic success and widen the gap between rich and poor.[15]

Table 7-1. *Segregation (Dissimilarity) of the Poor and of Blacks in Selected Metropolitan Areas*

Metropolitan area	Dissimilarity of poor, 1990	Change 1970–90	Dissimilarity of blacks, 1990	Change 1970–90
Atlanta	39.6	−0.2	67.8	−14.3
Chicago	49.8	8.3	85.8	−6.1
Dallas	37.3	−1	63.1	−23.8
Los Angeles	34.9	3.8	73.1	−17.9
Miami	31.3	−1.9	71.8	−13.3
New York	43	5	82.2	1.2
San Francisco	36	3	66.8	−13.3
Washington, D.C.	38.1	0.9	66.1	−15

Sources: Alan J. Abramson, Mitchell J. Tobin, and Matthew R. VanderGoot, "The Changing Geography of Metropolitan Opportunity: The Segregation of the Poor in U.S. Metropolitan Areas, 1970 to 1990," *Housing Policy Debate*, vol. 6, no. 1 (1993), pp. 45–72; and Douglas S. Massey and Nancy A. Denton, *American Apartheid: Segregation and the Making of the Underclass* (Harvard University Press, 1993), p. 222.

Those who feel threatened by poverty and color-creep have two options: to fort up in place or to move to a perceived safe zone and fortify themselves there. The wealthy who have homes in desirable locations, on the ocean or near downtown, can and do fortify their areas. Likewise, working- and middle-class people without the resources to move simply close or barricade their streets. But people of all classes are increasingly opting to move to a safety zone of new gated communities in the outer suburbs and exurbs.

At the same time, gated communities may be reinforcing people's fear. Dennis Judd has suggested that "the trappings of security that impregnate the new walled communities must [remind] the inhabitants, constantly and repetitively, that the world beyond their walls is dangerous."[16]

Safety is usually given as the overwhelming rationale for flight from the city, even though national data indicate that very few upper-middle-class whites have ever had any personal experience with violent crime. Nonetheless, the annual survey of predominantly upper-income suburban Orange County, California, conducted by Mark Baldassare indi-

Figure 7-2. *Reasons for Leaving Chicago*

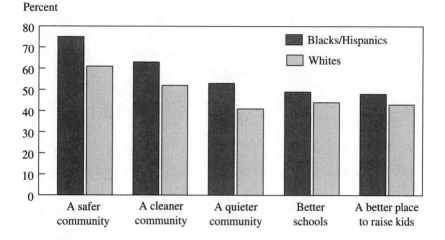

Source: "Reasons for Leaving," Moving Out series, *Chicago Tribune,* December 1, 1993.

cates that 44 percent of the residents there fear being the victim of a crime; 39 percent fear crime in public parks; and 31 percent fear crime in shopping malls. A Time/CNN poll found that 89 percent of Americans think crime is getting worse, while 55 percent worry about becoming a victim of crime.[17]

A graphic example of the crime and class issues confronting cities is contained in a *Chicago Tribune* survey on people's motivations for moving out of Chicago to the suburbs (see figure 7-2). Interviews from the *Chicago Tribune*'s series are typical and could be from any major metropolis. Said one respondent, "I wanted a large, fabulous house with a yard—and no poor people." Said another, "We became worn out by the traffic, parking hassles, noise, crime, lack of being able to feel safe, dirty streets, etc. We did not feel the City of Chicago was a good place to start a family."[18]

Fear is a powerful force that can overcome all reason. In fact, the rates of the most serious crimes have fallen, except for juvenile gang violence.[19] Nonetheless, the fear of becoming a victim of a crime even in one's own neighborhood or home is stimulating more defensive measures. As the nation's population is transformed, and as the suburbs fail to make real people's dream of escaping from crime, from the poor, and from inadequate city services, few feel secure. The perception is that crime has become more random, that all strangers are sources of danger, that no place is safe. Gating the neighborhood provides at least psychological relief from this fear. It provides an illusion of control and stability. It also allows those who can afford it to opt out of shared public services and public places with impunity.

Social Contact and the Social Contract

No community will ever be an island. But social and demographic data indicate a dividing nation; metropolitan areas are becoming increasingly spatially fragmented and segregated by race, class, and land values.[20] This fragmentation is also being seen on a much larger scale across the country.

One of the major demographic changes affecting our metropolitan areas has been the flow of immigrants. The sources of immigration have changed dramatically since the 1940s, when 70 percent of immigrants came from Europe. By 1993 that number had dwindled to 15 percent, with 44 percent of the immigrants coming from Latin America and the Caribbean.[21] The states where gated communities first took root, and where they now are most widespread, are also those where foreign immigration has been highest: California and Florida. Most of the unprecedented volume of foreign immigration in the 1980s was concentrated in seven states: New York, New Jersey, Illinois, Massachusetts, California, Texas, and Florida, all of which experienced significant white out-migration. Whites are now fleeing entire states and regions in the face of dramatic demographic change.[22] Many of the other states with large or growing numbers of gates, such as Arizona, Oregon, Washington, and Nevada, are destination states for the increasing numbers of white Californians fleeing the state. Gated areas are in part a response to this trend, representing a concrete metaphor for the closing of the gates against immigrants and minorities and the poverty, crime, and social instabilities in society at large.

In an essay on the racial tensions in Dana Point, California, where roughly one-third of the city is behind gates, writer Dale Maharidge tells how culture-clash and fear combine and harden into gated communities: "What do you do if you've worked all your life to buy a dream home, and suddenly the neighborhood becomes more dangerous? Even ardent liberals react when people get killed on their street. And what do you do if you're a hardworking, law-abiding immigrant who just wants to make a buck and better your life, but other people want you to get the hell out?" The problem he sees is one of "basically good people who do not understand each other."[23]

White and middle-class flight from the city, the inner suburbs, and even entire states, and walls built to help protect those who stay behind, leave poor neighborhoods increasingly isolated from municipal land, labor, and social markets and from the benefits of society as a whole. There is increasing evidence that the spatial isolation of minorities in itself reduces opportunities for these already most-vulnerable groups.[24] John Kain, a pioneer in studies of the effects of spatial discrimination, has argued that housing market discrimination leading to racial segregation is a major reason for the low employment levels of blacks in the central city.[25] William Julius Wilson's work reinforces this view, concluding that "the lack of sustained contact or social interaction with individuals and the institutions that represent the mainstream society . . . makes it much more difficult for those who are looking for jobs to be tied into the job network."[26]

Gated communities create yet another barrier to interaction among people of different races, cultures, and classes and may add to the problem of building the social networks that form the base for economic and social opportunity. Neighborhoods have always been able to exclude some potential residents through discrimination and housing costs. With gates and walls, they can exclude not only undesirable new residents, but even casual passersby and the people from the neighborhood next door. Gates are a visible sign of exclusion, an even stronger signal to those who already see themselves as excluded from the larger mainstream social milieu.

Despite efforts to interview an ethnically diverse set of gated-community residents, our focus groups and interviews in six different areas included not a single African American or Asian American and only one Latino. We did see African Americans in a couple of the developments, but they were clearly an extreme minority. The segregation that gated communities represent is intentionally economic, but race and class are closely correlated attributes in our society. Gated communities do not in themselves cause discrimination and residential segregation, but they are part of the pattern, with all its attendant effects on economic and social opportunity.

I've Got Mine: Exclusionary Policies

Gated communities exist to wall out crime or traffic or strangers as well as to lock in economic position. Greater control over the neighborhood is presumed to mean greater stability in property values. As discussed in chapter 1, there is no evidence that developer-built gated communities either command a price premium or maintain their values better than nongated communities. Nonetheless, the perception that gates can increase or help maintain property values is strong, and many residents and realtors believe they do have a positive impact. Neighborhood groups in California petitioning to gate off their streets admit to expecting property value increases of as much as 40 percent in ten years.[27]

The race to lock in position and equity makes sense for those behind the gates, but the results may affect their nearby neighbors adversely. Opponents of gated communities in Plano, Texas, claim that a gated community decreases property values in adjacent neighborhoods by 5 percent.[28] There is fear that excluding crime from one area will displace at least some of it to adjacent areas. Where gating reduces traffic for residents within, cars are diverted to streets on the outside.

Street barricades and gates can alter the patterns of the simple daily uses of public streets, such as parking and afternoon walks, by denying access to all but those who own property behind the obstruction. They prevent kids from the next subdivision from riding their bikes through; they may exclude Girl Scouts selling cookies and trick-or-treaters. And, of course, gates and barricades affect not only neighboring subdivisions but also the other citizens of a town or region. They keep out canvassers and campaigners, limiting the democratic process. Gates can make access to shorelines, beaches, and parks so difficult that those public resources become essentially private preserves.

In addition to gates, exclusionary zoning, no-growth policies, and other government actions are effective manifestations of the same trend to control space regardless of the effect on neighbors and neighboring jurisdictions. These policies and regulations are a supplementary mode of residential exclusion. They result in a pattern of segregation of race and of incomes. This pattern of segregation acts as a clear proxy for housing values, neighborhood quality, and other elements that go into producing the perception of value.[29]

Although we found no evidence that gates automatically increase or help maintain housing values, the perception that they do is an important reason they are spreading so rapidly. Likewise, the growing fear of the loss of housing value is recasting land use planning tools and giving rise to a new surge of land management efforts aimed at retarding population growth and maintaining high land and housing prices. No-growth zoning policy, for example, is not merely a land use regime but a bundle of policies that strongly influence residential composition. Land use policies are used to restrict lower-income entrants into a city. When combined with segregative and discriminatory practices in the public and private sectors and reduced federal funding for affordable housing, restrictive land use regimes do not just protect land and property values— they determine the geography of opportunity in a metropolitan area. As Rabin says,

> These diverse policies and activities differ widely in the nature and intensity of their impacts on economic and structural isolation of the poor. Some exert powerful influences on the spatial distribution of development; some influence the nature of development; while others establish conditions of access to the benefits of development. It is important to recognize those public policies that disproportionately increase the opportunity for whites to leave the central city.[30]

These "turf wars," dramatically manifested by the gated community, are a troubling trend in land use planning. As some citizens separate themselves into homogeneous, independent cells and their ties to the greater polity and society become attenuated, we may see increasing resistance to efforts to resolve some local municipal, let alone regional, problems. As they become more distant physically and psychologically from a changing nation, the potential for large-scale civic secession and withdrawal from the public realm grows. As one citizen told Constance Perin in her study of community and place in American life: "See, you have to understand the fundamental feeling in suburbia is fear, let's face it. The basic emotional feeling is fear. Fear of blacks, fear of physical harm, fear of their kids being subjected to drugs, which are identified as a black problem, fear of all the urban ills. They feel [that] by moving to the suburbs they've run away from it, in fact, they haven't, in reality they haven't, but in their own mind's eye they've moved away from the problem."[31]

As urban problems arise in the older inner-ring suburbs, fear spreads. Gated communities are no more a cause of this fragmentation and conflict in metropolitan areas than they are of racial segregation. Rather, they are again a manifestation of these larger social trends. On the macro level, better-off suburban cities and neighborhoods fight to keep their position, just as homeowners and housing developments do on the micro level.

Debating Gates

The effects that gates have on the people and places around them—symbolic and manifest, social and physical—are reasons for serious debate. Political representatives, civil servants, and the public need to consider both the narrow and the broad consequences of this new residential pattern. Among city officials and planners, most, like the planners in Palm Springs, take gated communities for granted, limiting their concerns to practical issues of traffic flow, aesthetics, and emergency vehicle access.[32] When we started the research for this book, very few localities were going beyond these concerns. Fortunately, more and more towns and cities are now making serious efforts to evaluate gates and their effects.

Recognizing the conflicts that can occur over gates, many localities have held hearings and developed guidelines for the approval of gated communities, especially those created through retrofitting. Addressing primarily the barricading and gating of public streets, cities and counties from Laguna Niguel, California, to Jefferson Parish, Louisiana, have set rules about traffic impact and neighborhood approval. Usually, a supermajority of 75 or 80 percent of residents must approve a closure, but some cities, like Dallas, Texas, require 100 percent resident approval. Sometimes debates are prompted when a neighborhood first petitions to close its streets; sometimes they occur when a city council or planning department realizes that gates are growing quickly in number.

Because most localities approve developers' gates as part of the standard permitting process, it is usually street barricades and the privatization of public streets that lead to lengthy debate and separate ordinances. Only a few cities have legal ordinances regulating gating, and even fewer govern developer-built gates as well as retrofits. The number of cities to concern themselves with all types of gated communities, however, is growing. In 1995, San Diego, California, and Portland, Oregon, began a process to establish a municipal policy on gates. One of the first to do so was Plano, Texas, a suburb on the border of North Dallas.

Plano is a rapidly growing town of nearly 200,000 people that saw its first gated subdivisions in the early 1990s. The city council grew concerned and placed a moratorium on gates until it could debate the issue and draft a policy. The council was worried about traffic circulation, connections between neighborhoods, the safety of neighboring subdivisions, the image of gates, and the danger of overconcentration. It conceived the debate as a discussion of the kind of city Plano was to become.

The council was divided on the issue, as were many of the citizens of Plano. Ann Jones, a member of the council and a realtor herself told us she believes "people should be able to drive on any street they choose." However, she went on to say, "It provides the illusion of safety, but nevertheless when you hear of drive-by shootings and all this in the news it's hard to argue that it won't help eliminate some of that."[33] In the end, the doubters triumphed in Plano: the guidelines passed in 1994 restrict gates to developments that already have natural barriers such as streams on three sides. At the time, there was only one undeveloped site in Plano that fit that description. Since then, at least two other towns in Texas, Keller and Southlake, have followed suit with their own moratoriums on gated communities.[34]

These policies and ordinances, especially when developed with substantial public input, are a highly useful and farsighted step for local governments to take. Planning should be used to knit a framework for a locality, and gates, as we have seen, have a major influence on issues from traffic circulation to crime to public services to community cohesion. These issues are easiest to see when an existing neighborhood petitions to privatize its streets, but they need to be examined just as closely when a new gated subdivision is proposed. Our research highlights the need for localities to seriously and carefully consider the many social issues surrounding gated communities.

The importance of this debate is seen in our field work in cities and suburbs, where those who espouse gates and barricades and those who oppose them are equally fervent. In Whitley Heights, people moved out over losing the battle to gate the area. In Miami Shores, some residents left because the barricades were put in and others because they were placed on someone else's street.

There are many concerned observers who object to the gating trend. Many in Los Angeles, including City Councilwoman Rita Walters, have objected to street closures, predicting a future of barricades and entry permits. Norman Krumholz, former planning director of Cleveland, Ohio, has warned of the potential for the balkanization of cities.[35] Still others question the wisdom of protecting limited areas without considering the effects on the city or region as a whole. And many worry about increasing segregation and racist motivations. Lexy McCulloch, a planner in Burr Ridge, Ohio, says that the planning commission opposes gates as "separatist" and has requested they be removed from at least one proposed development. She is also concerned about the less stringent right-of-way requirements for private streets and the possibility that future residents may ask the city to take over maintenance when street repairs become costly.[36] One of our focus group members in Dallas provided this sage comment: "What I wonder about the gated community is, what is going to happen twenty, thirty years from now? Will they be maintained? Down the road, if history repeats itself, that's going to become a middle-income, a lower-income area, maintenance is probably going to decline. What are we creating? Why are we creating a gated community? Nine out of ten times, it's just to keep different races or income groups out of the community."[37]

In Los Angeles, Atlanta, Chicago, Sacramento, and other cities, significant battles over proposals for street closures and gated communities have been fought in courts and city halls. In Wichita, Kansas, the debate over gating began when a public street subdivision petitioned the city council to be allowed to install a barrier arm gate at its entrance. The subdivision, called Gatewood, already had a guardhouse, manned at night, at the sole point of entry. There was a camera system that recorded the license plates of all cars entering the development. Because the streets are public, access could not be denied, but it could be monitored. The gate was intended to increase this monitoring ability. Residents would have remote controls to open the gate; nonresidents would have to stop and push a button, at which point another camera could photograph their faces.

The Metropolitan Area Planning Commission, the Traffic Commission, and the Office of Citizen Participation were asked for input. All voted to recommend that the city council deny permission. The Planning Department argued that "gates are a symbol of whether the City views itself as a 'civic association' or as a collection of enclaves." In its report, it noted "a trend for residents to protect their interests more and more vociferously when it comes to the threat of a zoning change in their 'backyards,' while it is becoming increasingly difficult to find public-spirited citizens to serve on boards and committees that deal with broader community-wide issues."[38] One Planning Commission member, who voted to recommend approval, suggested that it was not for those outside to tell the residents of Gatewood what to do, especially since they had come together to take action to improve their neighborhood. Another disagreed, saying that although the neighborhood's initiative was positive, there were "all kinds of things" neighborhoods could do "without having to gate themselves off from the rest of the community."[39]

The anti-gating organizations and individuals express a range of arguments, from the legal and bureaucratic to the social and philosophical. Common are expressions of the old notions of civic bondedness: "I love this community and I want to keep it clean and green and open, and you can't do that sitting behind a gate thumbing your nose at the world. I've seen enough bars and gates to last several lifetimes."[40] Some have a clear view of what it means to be a member of the civic community and see gates as establishing partitions between citizens: "The idea is divisive. This proposal is to gate a city within a city. I am not separate from the rest of Plant City and I don't want to be."[41]

A member of CAGE, the neighborhood group that started the long-running suit against Whitley Heights in Los Angeles, provided a strong statement of opposition, expressing how gated communities are magnifying differences instead of commonalities and creating different classes of citizenship: "It says 'stay out' and it also says, 'We are wealthy and you guys are not, and this gate shall establish the difference.'"[42]

Our case studies revealed in detail the position of those who support gates. Their reasons are a litany of the things everyone wants in a residential community: safety, peace, quiet, privacy. They believe that their right to control their environment goes beyond their front doors to the streets around them, and they argue that no one has the right to prevent them from exercising that control: "Birds of a feather flock together, and they have a right to do so. If that presents a problem to society, that's the way it is. If people who wish tight security wish to flock together, that's their business."[43]

Residents and proponents of gates deny charges of racism, elitism, and separatism. They say they are simply caring for their homes, their families, and their neighborhoods. And they are overwhelmingly content with their choice of gated communities. As a resident of the newly barricaded neighborhood of Five Oaks in Dayton, Ohio, exulted, "Traffic is absolutely nil. My wife and I sit on our porch in the summertime and say, 'This is the next best thing to living in the country.'"[44]

Safety to walk the streets day or night, the ability to protect property and one's investment in a home, good services and infrastructure—these attributes, which should be universal rights provided equally for all citizens, are what gated communities attempt to provide. But for reasons ranging from global forces to national policies to chronic lack of funds, our localities and cities fail to provide this basic quality of life. We cannot blame gated community residents for the problems of urban America or for their efforts to reduce the influence of those problems on themselves and their families. However, there are other ways to the same end. We examine some of the alternatives in chapter 8.

8

Building Better Communities

IN GATED communities across the nation, we heard people say they want to take their neighborhoods back. They want safety, they want quiet, and they want to feel secure. Though they do not often say so explicitly, they want community as well; they are pleased and proud when they feel they are part of a residential area that has a sense of community. Given these desires, the movement toward gates, guards, fences, walls, and concrete barricades is understandable. These physical security measures seem to offer protection and peace of mind. If they also divide neighborhood from neighborhood, encourage privatization, and send signals of exclusion, that may seem a small price to pay. Some residents of gated communities told us that their first obligation must be to look after their families, their blocks, and their neighborhoods before worrying about the rest of the world.

Yet there are alternatives to gates for both cities and suburbs that can help prevent crime, control traffic, and make neighborhoods livable. No method of crime or traffic control is always appropriate or completely successful, and we present these alternatives not as panaceas but as tactics that can achieve some of the same ends as gates without building barriers between neighborhoods and neighbors. These alternatives help protect and beautify the environment and give children safe places to play. At the same time they help build the social ties that are the basis for the shared values and mutuality of community. They work to build one or both of the two aspects of our definition of community—the "private" community of sentiment and the "public" community of shared destiny or goals and involvement in community affairs.

Because community is also the bedrock of healthy cities and regions, we also look at some ideas for promoting community beyond the local level. These include new design principles for towns and neighborhoods and regional approaches to problem solving. Good communities are important not just to individuals but to society and to the nation.

Creating Good Neighborhoods: Crime Prevention

Police, criminologists, urban planners, and architects have developed a wide range of physical design tactics to help reduce and control crime. Taken together, these security measures are called Crime Prevention through Environmental Design (CPTED). They range from physical design changes that create or facilitate the informal social behaviors that deter crime to "target-hardening" measures (a military term for armoring vulnerable points) that use physical barriers or technological surveillance. CPTED often employs the locks, bars, fences, razor wire, gates, and guards of basic target-hardening crime prevention, but it puts its primary emphasis on influencing social behavior.

The central idea is to create defensible space, a physical environment in which the neighborhood's social organization deters crime. Any physical changes that are made are intended to promote social defense, not to act directly against crime. The term "defensible space" was coined and most fully developed by Oscar Newman; similar ideas have been put forth by Jane Jacobs and others.[1] As Newman developed it, the theory rests on three propositions:

—territoriality: people are more likely to defend territory they identify as theirs;

—natural surveillance: the easier it is to observe a space and the more observers there are, the more criminals will be deterred; and

—image: visual characteristics can encourage or deter crime.[2]

Territoriality is created by using designs that incorporate easily claimed spaces—areas that are meant for small groups—rather than large, public expanses. Natural surveillance is achieved through elements such as window placement, lighting, and landscaping. Image is created using tactics that signal that a place is cared for, that it belongs to someone— good maintenance, removal of graffiti, encouraging the presence of people outside, and clearly marking boundaries.

In relation to gated communities, the concepts of territoriality and image apply. But the presence of gates themselves does not constitute defensible space or crime prevention through environmental design. The developer-built lifestyle and prestige communities are rarely intended as defensible space. Exclusion is not the same as protection, and fenced borders do not automatically create a community that will defend them. In the security zone, however, gated communities are sometimes designed to reflect defensible-space ideas; gates are usually accompanied by community organizing, cooperation with law enforcement, the formation of Neighborhood Watch groups, graffiti clean-up, and other nondesign tactics that fit the socially oriented defensible-space approach and have an independent effect on crime reduction.

Defensible-space approaches to security can and do strengthen community. Target-hardening approaches, when used alone, as they are in suburban gated communities, may help a neighborhood protect itself but rely on physical devices and barriers to do so instead of social controls. When neighborhoods rely on technological devices and hired guards for security, they weaken rather than strengthen their connectedness and nullify individuals' responsibility for the security of their neighbors.

We saw little evidence of a feeling of mutual responsibility in the developer-initiated gated communities we visited, although we did sometimes find evidence of such connectedness in existing neighborhoods that had mobilized to gate themselves off. In general, people perceived their developments as friendly but felt isolated in them. The young lawyer in Florida told us that at a development Christmas party he and his wife did not know anyone and felt no one really wanted to know them. Similarly, couples in Blackhawk, California, found that despite the interaction fostered through tennis and golf clubs, they did not feel connected. The essential mutuality of community is the missing ingredient. In gated communities, hired guards, club organizers, and external agents substitute for mutual responsibility.

Table 8-1. *Crime Prevention Tactics for Neighborhoods*[a]

Tactic	Physical	Managerial	Police	Social
Surveillance				
Increase outdoor lighting	x	...	...	...
Reduce blind spots	x	...	...	...
Install guard booths	x	...	...	...
Install surveillance cameras	x	...	...	...
Hire security guards	...	x	...	...
Form block watches	...	...	...	x
Form resident patrols	...	...	...	x
Arrange for police patrols	...	...	x	...
Create territorial space	x	...	...	...
Start house-sitting programs	...	...	...	x
Start safe-home programs	...	...	...	x
Create community policing	...	...	x	...
Movement control	...	...	...	...
Close or gate streets	x	...	...	...
Build fences and walls	x	...	...	...
Provide escort services	...	x	...	...
Get to know neighbors	...	...	...	x
Motivation reinforcement	...	...	...	...
Improve appearance	x	...	...	...
Personalize the environment	x	...	...	...
Use minimum security codes	...	x	...	...
Provide education programs	...	...	...	x
Get residents involved	...	...	...	x
Improve police-community relations	...	...	x	...

Source: Adapted from Allan Wallis and Daniel Ford, *Crime Prevention through Environmental Design* (Washington, D.C.: National Institute of Justice, U.S. Department of Justice, 1981).

a. Community-building tactics are in italics.

But there are many choices for security and crime prevention other than hired guards and concrete walls. Table 8-1 lists tactics that CPTED uses to increase security in residential neighborhoods. Many are purely physical changes, and some depend on law enforcement agencies. Others rely on social ties and the organization of neighbors, because CPTED is based on the idea of promoting social interaction. Physical designs are intended to trigger social mechanisms and so are often implemented in tandem with social tactics.

Target-hardeners such as fences, walls, gates, and security patrols are one range of options. From the point of view of building community, these may help stabilize and provide a base for neighborhood, but they do not in themselves guarantee community. And as we have discussed, they can damage it by relieving residents of personal responsibility for their neighbors.

The community-building tactics listed in table 8-1 may be used alone or together with physical target-hardening and law enforcement tactics. They bring people together and enable and encourage neighbors to look out for each other and to care for their environment. Gerda Wekerle and Carolyn Whitzman have argued for a "Safe Cities" approach, which integrates physical design and resident involvement to fight crime and reduce fear. Referring to the "territoriality" aspect of CPTED, they note that "attempts to encourage 'pride of place' are not dependent on design alone, but relate to the opportunity people have to participate in the design, planning, and management of those places."[3] Also, community-building tactics improve the quality of life as well as increase security. Examples include Neighborhood Watch programs and resident patrols that bring neighbors together and provide security; programs that establish safe houses where neighborhood children know they can always go for help; programs and events that acquaint neighbors with each other so they can identify strangers and suspicious activity more readily; the improvement of the appearance of the neighborhood; and the involvement of children, teenagers, and adults in these efforts to increase neighborhood pride and give everyone a stake in the community.

Unlike fences, gates, and guards, which can be bought and paid for and delegated to someone else to manage, all of these community-building efforts take time, administration, monitoring, and follow-through and almost always fall to overworked volunteer neighborhood activists. In some neighborhoods around the country, a new answer to the problem of volunteer burnout has been developed: hire a paid "community coach." The coach is a full- or part-time person, preferably a community member, who coordinates the neighborhood efforts. Acknowledging that police can't do it all, churches, homeowner associations, merchant associations, and other groups in hundreds of places can put their money not into hardware but into the position of a dedicated community leader who spearheads crime prevention programs and coordinates volunteers.[4]

The community pride and cohesion these tactics can provide is demonstrated in the Mount Pleasant neighborhood in Washington, D.C. Mount Pleasant is a working-class neighborhood of blacks, whites, and Latino and Asian immigrants. Crime had been a problem of long standing in the area; but after a race-based riot in 1991 and a series of drive-by shootings in 1993 that left three people dead, the neighborhood mobilized. Residents began to meet regularly with police about their concerns; a Neighborhood Watch program was started; and a massive block party was held to celebrate the spirit of the effort to improve the neighborhood. "We wanted to take our community into our own hands. I'd rather get the community together than get up and leave," one man told a reporter. Said another, "After all those things happened in Mount Pleasant, we are still together. What happened made the neighborhood strong."[5]

Community-building CPTED tactics are intended to recreate the social order of the neighborhoods and small towns of decades past— neighborhoods where people knew each other and watched out for each other, where there were many eyes on the street and mischievous teenagers and malicious criminals found it hard to escape detection. Locks, fences, and gates remind people of danger and fear; but like the small town or the stable city neighborhood of the fondly remembered past, a tightly knit community empowers, reassures, and improves the quality of life as it increases security.

Creating Good Neighborhoods: Traffic Control

Traffic is the second major reason that neighborhoods turn to gates and fences. Residents dislike the noise and disruption of through-traffic, they worry about their children playing in the streets, they fear that easy automobile access gives criminals free entrance and quick escapes. Again, a wide variety of tactics can be employed to control traffic without locking out the world.

Some of these techniques are old standbys like speed bumps, raised dots, and curving streets. Newer ideas include crosswalks raised to the level of sidewalks or raised intersections, both of which act as a sort of speed bump, and sharper corners to create smaller turning diameters. All of these slow traffic, thereby increasing safety, decreasing noise, and reducing the volume of through-traffic. Other measures facilitate

A slow street: Walnut Hollow, Colorado
John M. Fernandez

community at the same time that they control traffic, like the best of the crime prevention tactics. Many of these techniques are part of the new urbanists' vision for suburban developments and redesigned city neighborhoods that work as communities—as both social and physical spaces.

The central model of this new vision of street design is called traffic calming, street integration, or shared streets. The idea originated in Europe in the 1960s and has been widely, and successfully, adopted in the Netherlands, Germany, England, Denmark, Sweden, Japan, Israel, Switzerland, and Australia.[6] It is only now being implemented in the United States.[7]

The idea of shared streets is simple: make residential streets into spaces that serve all the people who use them—not just drivers but also pedestrians, residents, and children. Depending on the volume of traffic the street must accommodate, a range of elements may be used to calm traffic. Shared streets are narrowed to slow traffic and reduce the streets' visual impact. They curve or zigzag, they have no sidewalks, and the surface is paved in brick or cobblestone rather than asphalt, signaling that the space is for pedestrians as well as cars. On-street parking is interspersed with trees and other landscaping. Sometimes benches and other street furniture are incorporated.

On a residential street with no through-traffic, there is no need for twenty-five-mile-per-hour speeds. Speed limits of five miles per hour are adequate, along with parking and garage access. These streets are sometimes designed as queuing streets: they have sections wide enough for only one car, so that drivers must slow and take turns for a clear lane. A variety of designs and materials are available that preserve emergency vehicle access. Where space is taken away from cars, it is given to the children and pedestrians for whom the street becomes safe and pleasant, an extension of their own front yards.

Studies of shared streets in Europe indicate increased play activity by children and dramatically fewer traffic accidents.[8] Whether the street is a true shared street or just incorporates some of the elements depends on the needs of traffic, residents, and pedestrians. Whatever the degree of traffic calming desired, all of these measures can be incorporated into new subdivisions, and most can be adapted to existing streets in city grids.

Some North American cities have imported the shared-streets idea in the 1990s. Boulder, Colorado, has built planned-unit developments incorporating shared streets, and the city is restructuring its street design standards to allow the wider application of the model. Santa Fe, New Mexico, is also reviewing new design guidelines, and Portland, Oregon; Olympia, Washington; and Vancouver, British Columbia have already adopted new standards.[9]

The effect of integrated street design on traffic has added benefits for crime prevention. Because shared streets increase the use of public spaces, there is greater social interaction, more eyes on the street. And they work as defensible spaces by marking territory and sending signals that increase residents' sense of ownership. Most important, they accomplish the same objectives as street barricades without actually closing off access. Gates and barricades are used to close streets, to slow cars, and to prevent through-traffic. Slow streets do the same but do not exclude anyone, and they have the additional benefits of facilitating informal social control and encouraging community.

Community Building and Sustainable Communities

Community-building is a hot concept in the development business, from gated subdivisions marketed as "communities" to entire planned cities promoted as "your new hometown." The master-planned towns built by the Irvine Company started this trend, using physical design descended from Ebenezer Howard's Garden City. They have shown us that physical design and planning influence behavior and social structure, and they affect how residents feel. The design of new residential developments, whether in suburbs or cities, can bring people together rather than divide and separate them. Similarly, the redevelopment or even simple improvement of existing neighborhoods can be used to build community and strengthen it. Planners, architects, and citizens across the country are trying to create what they call sustainable communities.

Sustainable communities bring together concern for the environment, social justice, public life, and private life. They are sustainable in that they do not simply meet the needs of people today but also consider the ability of their residents' children and grandchildren to meet their own needs in the future. Hallmarks of sustainable design include more compact development, environmental protection, citizen participation in design and implementation, equal access to services, concern for all members of the community, public spaces to bring people together, and architecture and zoning that promote a sense of place.[10]

Gated communities are rarely designed to fulfill these goals. They intentionally lack flexibility. They emphasize strong covenants, conditions, and restrictions (CC&Rs), which make adaptive reuse difficult, and perhaps impossible. They attempt to protect the future by reifying the past. They employ walls and guards to prevent crime rather than applying integrated, holistic solutions that encourage community participation to ward off destructive elements. Gated communities do not undertake strategies to acquire and maintain adequate education, jobs, and public services—fundamental civic goals that are the first crucial step in crime prevention.[11] Instead of rich and vibrant public spaces, they contain, at best, private recreational facilities and clubhouses that serve a limited membership and offer a narrow range of activities rather than the entire spectrum of community needs.

It must be said that we found a more enlightened perspective among some individuals and in some places. In the large gated city of Canyon Lake, California, town leaders are working hard to achieve community integration and to build communal participation and problem-solving efforts. But most gated communities are sealed-off suburban subdivisions, part of a sprawling and unconnected environment that wastes human and physical resources, cuts off links between neighboring developments, and fragments and separates all forms of indigenous community formation. For those who share the vision of sustainable communities, the gating trend ignores the very elements of communities that make them places that will endure, places to remember, to care for, and to call home.

One notable vision of sustainable community is neotraditionalism, which tries to recreate the best of the traditional American town. Even in the suburbs, there is a long design tradition in this country of development that does not sprawl, is pedestrian-friendly, and encourages community, contact, and a small-town feeling.[12] The street patterns of traditional American towns provided privacy and security without barriers. Privacy was provided by layers of space, which were created by narrow streets, trees, semi-public front spaces like porches and stoops, and security through the eyes-on-the-street mechanisms of social control. People were still segregated by income and race into different areas, but at least they were accessible to each other and shared public spaces.

Phil Langdon, a widely read urban author and reporter, defines neotraditionalism as connection—between streets, between residential and retail uses, between incomes and housing types, and also through mass transit, public spaces, and especially civic ideals and public responsibilities.[13] Of the architects and planners who design and build neotraditional developments, Peter Calthorpe, Andres Duany, and Elizabeth Plater-Zyberk are the best known. Their developments have several characteristics in common: they are pedestrian-friendly with a mixed-use core and significant public space, and their design is intended to invoke a sense of tradition.[14]

The principles that neotraditionalism, the new urbanism, and the sustainable communities movements have given us point to many ways that gated communities are an inadequate and flawed means of reaching laudable ends. Everyone wants unified, active communities and to feel a sense of belonging and neighborliness. But the common reasons that people give for moving into suburban gated communities or gating off their urban neighborhoods are more prosaic. They are worried about their immediate quality of life, crime, control of their streets, traffic, and the safety of their children. Gates seem an effective and direct way to exclude strangers, wall out crime, and keep the speed and volume of traffic at safe levels.

Grid Street System
C. Benton

To many proponents of neotraditionalism, gated communities are the antithesis of their vision. For Peter Calthorpe they are manifestations of the growing imbalance between public and private space in American cities and neighborhoods:

> The gated community is perhaps the most blatant and literal expression of the trend [toward increased private space and the disappearance of public space]. Physically it denotes the separation, and sadly the fear, that has become the subtext of a country once founded on differences and tolerance. Politically it expresses the desire to privatize, cutting back the responsibilities of government to provide services for all and replacing it with private and focused institutions: private schools, private recreation, private parks, private roads, even quasi-private governments. Socially, the house fortress represents a self-fulfilling prophecy. The more isolated people become and the less they share with others unlike themselves, the more they do have to fear. To this extent privatization is a powerful force in the marketplace which directs the home building industry and our land use patterns.[15]

Critics have questioned the feasibility of neotraditionalism, its reliance on physical design to produce social behavior, and the degree to which it really works to create community and reduce stress on the environment. Nevertheless, there is much we can learn from neotraditional design principles in creating and recreating neighborhoods, making them better, safer, friendlier, and more livable places. These principles are simple yet powerful. They include bringing back the corner store, trading front lawns for more public open space, putting a porch at the front of the home and the garage in back, and making streets narrow and tree-lined, pedestrian-friendly. All of these ideas and many others like them focus on improving neighborhoods and towns and building new places that do not repeat the mistakes of the past. They lead to answers to our urban and suburban problems that do not rely on the hardware of gates and walls.

Creating Better Regions to Build Better Communities

Our towns and neighborhoods exist within regional metropolitan economic systems; they both shape and are shaped by the region of which they are part. Since the 1980s central cities have shrunk in population while metropolitan areas have gained population and grown dramatically in geographic size. The results of this regional restructuring are seen in every major city. Suburbs are less interested in cooperation or cohabitation with big cities. They have taken on their own municipal armor and often resist incorporation with their neighboring suburbs, nearby major cities, or larger regional entities. And as the suburbs differentiate, as older areas decay and the exurbs expand, competition and conflict arise between suburbs as well as between suburb and city. Mark Baldassare, one of the nation's foremost authorities on suburbs, has suggested that these trends will have major consequences:

> The affluent and organized [suburban] communities will do well. They will deliver services and attract revenues with greater success than others. Residents who can will move to the "successful" areas and thus raise the status and prospects of those advantaged places. Further inequalities in status, goods, and services will evolve. Some suburban communities will gain in overall quality while others will lose. Where

one lives and works in suburbia will become increasingly more important than whether one lives in the suburbs.[16]

Why is this important to our consideration of gated communities? Because all neighborhoods, gated and nongated, have the same ultimate goals: to control traffic, eliminate crime, protect economic position, and maintain a stable quality of life. On the level of the individual household, gating is a rational choice. But from the perspective of the city, the region, or the nation, gating does nothing to address the cause of the problems that it is a response to.

We must face the problems of poverty, social disorder, and failing municipal services and infrastructure rather than simply flee from them or wall them out. Our neighborhoods, our streets, our homes, and our families will never be truly safe while we ignore the greater community of which we are part. The structure and health of a region as a whole has a central role in determining economic and social opportunity as well as the quality of neighborhood life for all its residents. Part of a regional perspective is the acknowledgment that no neighborhood or locality stands alone, that the physical design of a neighborhood and the land use patterns we develop affect others in the region. The neighborhoods, towns, and cities that make up a region are interdependent.

Although we sympathize with the arguments on both sides, we believe that the entire civic realm must be considered when gating or barricading. Gating out the traffic or the drugs may pacify a neighborhood in the short term, but it may also lead to lack of interest in developing real solutions to those problems and others. And in the long term, the problems will encroach again. At the same time, no one should be subjected to intolerable traffic burdens and local criminality, and effective means must be found to mitigate them. The entire city needs to be involved in gating and barricading decisions because the larger community bears much of the physical and social burden the gates and barricades create. Such decisions require regional input as well, so that the effects of barriers on other jurisdictions become part of the information upon which the decisions are based.

In *New Visions for Metropolitan America*, Anthony Downs calls for a regional spirit of community. He points out that "no jurisdiction is an island. Every suburb is linked to its central city and to other suburbs. Therefore policymaking arrangements that do not consider the welfare of people who may be significantly affected by the policies created are not morally legitimate." Noting that this ideal is seldom met, because we define our communities and our responsibilities to them too narrowly, he concludes that "[this] situation violates the basic axiom of democracy stated in the Declaration of Independence that 'governments . . . derive their just powers from the consent of the governed.' Everyone who is significantly affected by public policy has a right to have a voice in determining that policy."[17] Community, as defined by Downs, is both a geographic entity and a sense of social responsibility. Gating, growth controls, and other forms of locality-based social separation are used to perpetuate and mask social and economic segregation. But it is becoming increasingly clear that actions on the metropolitan level can reduce this social and physical stress.

Regional councils of government (COGs) in a few parts of the country, such as the Bay Area Council in the San Francisco Bay Area and the Allegheny Conference of greater Pittsburgh, are paying attention to the wider social and land use issues tied to regional development. These bodies and others like them examine regional needs and forge new alliances for the benefit of the whole area. A regional transportation system in Portland, Oregon, has produced livable neighborhoods along its routes by developing the transit line around walkable "pedestrian pockets" to facilitate good neighborhood organization and development. Nongovernmental organizations such as BRIDGE Housing Corporation in San Francisco, which creates new housing and community living for residents of the San Francisco Bay Area, offer testimony to the effectiveness of regional solutions.[18] All of these efforts are designed to pull together political, social, and economic leadership to benefit all localities in the region.

But solutions, local or regional, will not be completely successful without a renewed federal commitment to our cities. Poverty and inequality may be exacerbated and perpetuated by the actions and nonactions of our local governments, but they are also shaped by national and global economic forces that can only be addressed by the federal government. The 1980s and 1990s have marked a dramatic retreat by Washington from antipoverty programs, including housing, health care, and education. Without these, and without a comprehensive economic policy aimed at increasing opportunity and reducing growing wealth and income disparities, local government efforts will be hamstrung.[19]

Divided We Fall

This book is about more than places with gates. It is about people. People make places and people erect gates against other people. Gates, walls, and security guards are being used by a growing number of Americans in reaction to the transformation of the nation's economy and society. These gates are real, but they are also a metaphor: gated communities are the protected zones on the battlefield where the internal ideological war over the American dream is played out.

In the 1960s, Daniel Patrick Moynihan wrote about the decline of the African American family and described the family structure as the transmitter of values and the entry point to the American economic system.[20] African Americans decried the Moynihan description of family disarray, but the issues he raised were prophetic with respect to the socioeconomic progress of black Americans. Today the family structure that Moynihan used as the backdrop for his work is scarcely recognizable in any American ethnic group.

As the family has crumbled, the community has become an increasingly important element in nation building. Americans no longer expect or trust that the family will be a strong, effective, and reliable bridge between the individual and society. Contemporary social philosophers, political leaders, and writers have called for the reaffirmation of community as the new cornerstone for the nation.[21] In a mobile and fragmented nation, community has become the anchor point for developing values, creating political responsibility, and forming social networks for employment and citizenship. As Michael Walzer said so eloquently, "The community is itself a good—conceivably the most important good—that gets distributed. But it is a good that can only be distributed by taking people in, where all the senses of that latter phrase are relevant; they must be physically admitted and politically received."[22]

Community has reentered the national lexicon because there are so few forces that bind the nation together. According to Anthony Downs, "In the long run America must strengthen the bases for its continued unity as a society by placing much more emphasis on social solidarity and less on individualistic needs."[23] But the way community is formed is as important as the goal itself. As we see this new fortress settlement pattern developing, we wonder if it will add to the democratic ideals we seek.

Community is part of American political myth and tradition, from the town meetings of New England to the barnraisings of the American frontier. Community in this tradition recognizes that individual lives and the futures of local places are indivisibly joined to their cities, regions, and nation. We must protect our neighborhood communities because they are essential and fundamental to our democratic society. Yet protecting houses and physical possessions with gates and guards is contradictory to community building on a broader level. It is the mutual support and shared social relationships of community that require protection and deserve our material and intellectual resources, not the symbols of separatism and alienist consumption.

The question for America is whether the nation can overcome its internal divisions and create a community across divisions of race, class, and culture, a true democracy with equality for all. We must restore the ideal of the broader community before we can restore the societal order that brings comfort and allows every American to contribute to the social well-being of the nation.

The fabric of civitas, communal commitment to civic and public life, has begun to rip. The damage grows with increasing privatization, increasing atomization, and increasing localism. The borders of the gated communities are emblematic of the proliferation of boundaries being set and hardened as communities fragment, looking inward. The need for others in society is lessening, and walls preventing contact are spreading.

Democracy is based in part on mutuality and collective citizenship, with the structure of communities tying individuals together across their dissimilarities to form a city, a region, and a nation. We now ask, can a nation survive and flourish without inclusive communities to undergird the practice of citizenship? Can the nation have any wholeness when communities are fragmented and pitted against each other socially, politically, and economically?

Franklin Roosevelt made a most profound statement of our need for collective destiny in 1936: "To some generations much is given. Of other generations much is expected. This generation of Americans has a rendezvous with destiny." Eric Goldman added that, for all of us, "To a large extent [social reform has been] the heart and the mind of the only nation in man's history which has dared to live by the credo that an individual's rendezvous with his destiny is a rendezvous with a better tomorrow."[24] Working out how we live together is our rendezvous with destiny and the only thing that will make America a truly better place, today and tomorrow.

When privatization and exclusion become dominant, and neighborhood connectedness and mutual support structures disappear, we must question whether an American democracy founded on citizenship and community remains possible. Abraham Lincoln said that "a house divided against itself cannot stand." Just as certainly, a nation that cannot achieve its ideals cannot offer much to itself or to the world. All of the walls of prejudice, ignorance, and economic and social inequality must come down before we can rendezvous with our democratic ideals. The walls of the mind must open to accept and cherish a more diverse nation. Then the walls that separate our communities, block social contact, and weaken the social contract will also come down.

Appendix

Survey of Homeowner Associations

WE DEVELOPED the following questions, which the Community Associations Institute included in its 1995 general survey of homeowner associations. The survey was mailed to approximately 7,000 boards of directors of CAI member associations across the country. The respondents were both residents of the communities and the elected representatives of those communities. These questions were in a separate section for gated communities only.

1. How important do you think the issue of security has been in the ultimate decision of residents to live in your community?

    ___ Unimportant

    ___ Somewhat important

    ___ Very important

    ___ Not sure

2a. How would you describe the level of community feeling in your development?

___ Neighborly and tight-knit

___ Friendly

___ Distant or private

2b. Compared to most communities in your area, would you say this is

___ Less neighborly

___ About the same

___ More neighborly

___ Not sure

3a. How would you describe the level of involvement of residents in your association government?

___ Very active

___ Somewhat active

___ Not very active

3b. How would you describe the level of involvement of residents in association-sponsored activities other than governance (i.e., social or charitable events)?

___ Very active

___ Somewhat active

___ Not very active

Notes

Chapter One

1. Definitive numbers on gated communities are unavailable. The difficulty is complicated by the rapidly increasing numbers, the lack of any national or state level data, and the lack of firm data even on the number of community associations. This rough estimate is based on the Community Association Institute's (CAI) estimated number of community associations. The CAI estimated that there were 150,000 community associations in 1952, with a growth rate of about 10,000 per year, giving 190,000 in 1996. According to the CAI, 52 percent of all community associations comprise single or attached dwellings arranged on streets. According to a recent survey of CAI member community associations on which we collaborated, 19 percent of community associations are gated. This gives a total of 18,772 developments that fit our definition of gated communities. Using the median number of units in gated communities from the survey, 166, we arrive at the estimate of 3,116,000 households behind gates. Multiplying by average household size of 2.7, this represents 8.4 million people. The estimate may be biased upward because of the tendency of larger developments to join the CAI, but at the same time the estimate does not include the significant and growing numbers of street closure situations.

2. Rowland Parker, *The Common Stream* (London: Granada Publishing, 1976).

3. Oscar Newman, *Community of Interest* (Garden City, N.Y.: Anchor Press/Doubleday, 1980).

4. See note 1 for details on how this estimate was made.

5. Interview with Marta Borsanyi, Robert Charles Lesser and Company, November 27, 1993.

6. Jim Carlton, "Behind the Gate: Walling Off the Neighborhood Is a Growing Trend," *Los Angeles Times,* October 8, 1989, sec. I, p. 3.

7. Data from *Residential Trends*, cited in ibid.

8. David W. Myers, "Today's Home Buyers Older Than in 70s," *Los Angeles Times,* June 17, 1990, sec. K, p. 2.

9. Andrew I. Kaplan, "Gatehouses in Demand at New Housing Complexes," *New York Times*, May 12, 1991, sec. 12, p. 1.

10. See Charles Hayes, "City Enclaves: Self-Contained Neighborhoods Dominate New Development," *Chicago Tribune*, June 12, 1993; Jim Sulski, "Security Is a Safe Way to Sell New Residences," *Chicago Tribune*, May 6, 1989, sec. 3, p. 3; Douglas A. Blackmon, "Well-to-Do Say Development Builds Barriers," *Atlanta Constitution*, December 17, 1992, sec. E, p. 1; and Deborah Royston. "Home Security Systems Are Growing in Popularity," *Atlanta Constitution*, July 7, 1991, sec. H, p. 3.

11. Michael Southworth and Eran Ben-Joseph, *Streets and the Shaping of Towns and Cities* (New York: McGraw Hill, 1997).

12. Robert Fishman, *Bourgeois Utopias: The Rise and Fall of Suburbia* (Basic Books, 1987), chapter 2.

13. Robert A. M. Stern, ed., *The Anglo-American Suburb*. Architectural Design Profile (New York: St. Martin's Press, 1981).

14. Kenneth Jackson, *Crabgrass Frontier: The Suburbanization of the United States* (New York: Oxford University Press, 1985).

15. Stern, ed., *The Anglo-American Suburb*, p. 19.

16. Rosabeth Moss Kanter, *Commitment and Community: Communes and Utopias in Sociological Perspective* (Harvard University Press, 1972), p. 54.

17. Stern, ed. *The Anglo-American Suburb*.

18. James Boswell, *Boswell's Life of Johnson* (London: H. Frowde, 1904).

19. Jackson, *Crabgrass Frontier.*

20. Christopher B. Leinberger, "Suburbia" (Robert Charles Lesser and Co., 1993).

21. Carlton, "Behind the Gate."

22. Interview with Steve Harvill, national consultant on gated communities, in Dallas, Texas, November 29, 1994.

23. Interview with Ami Tanel, Avatar Development Corporation, December 12, 1994.

24. Harvill interview.

25. Evan McKenzie, *Privatopia: Homeowner Associations and the Rise of Residential Private Government* (Yale University Press, 1994). McKenzie details Howard's rationale for the physical, economic, and social organization of the planned new town.

26. Ebenezer Howard quoted in ibid., p. 6.

27. Ibid., chap. 2.

28. HOAs are also referred to as community associations (CAs), residential community associations (RCAs), or common interest developments (CIDs).

29. Marc A. Weiss, "Community Builders and Community Associations: The Role of Real Estate Developers in Private Residential Governance," in *Residential Community Associations: Private Governments in the Intergovernmental System* (Washington, D.C.: United States Advisory Commission on Intergovernmental Relations, 1989).

30. In California these are called Mello-Roos bonds and are issued to cover the cost of infrastructure for a housing development at tax-exempt rates. A special district is established at the same time the housing development is built, with a set period of time in which to pay off the bonds. Such bonds are usually not highly rated, but because they are local government bonds they are easily marketed—or they were before the Orange County bankruptcy of 1995.

31. *Village of Belle Terre* v. *Boraas* (1974), quoted in Robert H. Nelson, "Private Neighborhoods: A New Direction for the Neighborhood Movement," in Charles C. Geisler and Frank J. Popper, eds., *Land Reform American Style* (Totowah, N.J.: Rowman and Allanheld, 1984), p. 321.

32. Doreen Heisler and Warren Klein, *Inside Look at Community Association Homeownership: Facts and Perceptions* (Alexandria, Va.: Community Associations Institute, 1996), pp. 7–8.

33. Community Associations Institute, *Community Associations Factbook* (Alexandria, Va.: Community Associations Institute, 1993).

34. Robert B. Reich, *The Work of Nations: Preparing Ourselves for 21st-Century Capitalism* (A. A. Knopf, 1991). See also McKenzie, *Privatopia;* Stanley Scott, "The Homes Association: Will 'Private Government' Serve the Public Interest?" *Public Affairs Report,* vol. 8, no. 1; United States Advisory Commission on Intergovernmental Relations, *Residential Community Associations: Private Governments in the Intergovernmental System?* (Washington, D.C.: USACIR, 1989); and Stephen E. Barton and Carol J. Silverman, "Common Interest Communities: Private Government and the Public Interest Revisited," in Stephen E. Barton and Carol J. Silverman, eds., *Common Interest Communities: Private Government and the Public Interest* (Institute of Governmental Studies Press, University of California at Berkeley, 1994).

35. See McKenzie, *Privatopia*; Earl Latham, "The Body Politic of the Corporation," in Edward S. Mason, ed., *The Corporation in Modern Society* (Harvard

University Press, 1959); and Sanford A. Lakoff with Daniel Rich, *Private Governments: Introductory Readings* (Glenview, Ill.: Scott, Foresman, 1973).

36. David J. Kennedy, "Residential Associations as State Actors: Regulating the Impact of Gated Communities on Nonmembers," *Yale Law Journal,* vol. 105, no. 3 (December 1995), pp. 761–93.

37. John E. Petersen, "The Blossoming of Microgovernments," *Governing* (October 1994), p. 78.

38. Robert J. Dilger, *Neighborhood Politics: Residential Community Associations in American Governance* (New York University Press, 1992); and Kennedy, "Residential Associations as State Actors."

39. Lucy Soto, "Suburban Fortresses: Gated Communities Are Going Up, Keeping Out," *Atlanta Constitution*, September 17, 1995, sec. F, p. 4.

40. Kevin V. Johnson, "Chicago Suburb a Fortress against Crime," *USA Today*, July 6, 1995, p. 3A.

41. John M. Glionna, "Hidden Hills Likes Its Politics out of View," *Los Angeles Times*, April 11, 1994, sec. A, p. 1.

42. Trevor Boddy, "Underground and Overhead: Building Analogous City," and Mike Davis, "Fortress Los Angeles: The Militarization of Urban Space," both in Michael Sorkin, ed., *Variations on a Theme Park: The New American City and the End of Public Space* (New York: Hill and Wang, 1992). Also see Richard Louv, *America II: The Book That Captures America in the Act of Creating the Future* (New York: Penguin, 1985).

43. Boddy, "Underground and Overhead," p. 151.

Chapter Two

1. Peter Marcuse, "Not Chaos, but Walls: Postmodernism and the Partitioned City," in Sophie Watson and Katherin Gibson, eds., *Postmodern Cities and Spaces* (Oxford: Blackwell, 1995), p. 248.

2. Ferdinand Tönnies, *Community and Society*, trans. and ed. C. P. Loomis (1887; reprint, New York: Harper, 1957).

3. Robert E. Park, Ernest W. Burgess, and Roderick D. McKenzie, *The City* (University of Chicago Press, 1925).

4. Louis Wirth, "Urbanism as a Way of Life," *American Journal of Sociology,* vol. 44 (1938), pp. 3–24.

5. Roland L. Warren, *The Community In America* (Chicago: Rand McNally, 1978).

6. Morris Janowitz, *Community Press in an Urban Setting: The Social Elements of Urbanism*, 2d ed. (University of Chicago Press, 1967).

7. Gerald Suttles, *The Social Construction of Communities* (University of Chicago Press, 1972).

8. Robert A. Nisbet, *The Quest for Community* (New York: Oxford University Press, 1970).

9. Melvin Webber, "Order in Diversity: Community without Propinquity," in Lowdon Wingo Jr., ed., *Cities and Space: The Future Use of Urban Land,* essays from the Fourth RRF Forum (Johns Hopkins University Press, 1963).

10. Barry Wellman and Barry Leighton, "Networks, Neighborhoods and Communities: Approaches to the Study of the Community Question," *Urban Affairs Quarterly,* vol. 14, no. 3 (1978), pp. 363–90; and Claude S. Fischer, *To Dwell among Friends: Personal Networks in Town and City* (University of Chicago Press, 1982).

11. George A. Hillery, Jr., "Definitions of Community: Areas of Agreement," *Rural Sociology,* vol. 20 (June 1955), p. 118.

12. Stephen E. Barton and Carol J. Silverman, *Common Interest Homeowners' Association Management Study* (Sacramento: California Department of Real Estate, 1987); Robert J. Dilger, *Neighborhood Politics: Residential Community Associations in American Governance* (New York University Press, 1992).

13. Dilger, *Neighborhood Politics,* p. 111.

14. Gregory S. Alexander, "Conditions of 'Voice': Passivity, Disappointment, and Democracy in Homeowner Associations," in Stephen E. Barton and Carol J. Silverman, eds., *Common Interest Communities: Private Government and the Public Interest* (Institute of Governmental Studies Press, University of California at Berkeley, 1994).

15. Gregory S. Alexander, "Dilemmas of Group Autonomy: Residential Associations and Community," *Cornell Law Review,* vol. 75, no. 1 (1989), pp. 1–61.

16. Herbert J. Gans, *The Levittowners: Ways of Life and Politics in a New Suburban Community* (Pantheon Books, 1967); Elijah Anderson, *Streetwise: Race, Class and Change in an Urban Community* (University of Chicago Press, 1990).

17. William Julius Wilson, *The Truly Disadvantaged: The Inner City, the Underclass, and Public Policy* (University of Chicago Press, 1987).

18. Robert Bellah and others, *Habits of the Heart: Indiviualism and Commitment in American Life* (Harper and Row, 1986).

19. Andres Duany and his partner Elizabeth Platter-Zyberck, along with Peter Calthorpe and several other nationally recognized architects, have been at the forefront of proposing pedestrian-oriented new towns that do not require gates or barricades but depend on residential design to promote a secure environment.

Chapter Three

1. Paul Richter, "It Just Seems Like We're Worse Off," *Los Angeles Times,* January 26, 1995, sec. A, p. 1.

2. Economic and Statistics Administration, *Sixty-Five Plus in the United States* (Washington, D.C.: Census Bureau, U.S. Department of Commerce, 1995).

3. Kevin Sullivan, "Folks Find Life at Leisure World Still Busy after All These Years," *Washington Post*, September 29, 1991, sec. B, p. 1.

4. Advertisement in the *Chicago Tribune*, May 6, 1989.

5. Lesley Alderman, "Four-Income Families," *Money*, vol. 24, no. 2 (February 1995), pp. 148–54.

6. Quoted in John O'Dell, "Par Excellence: Country Clubs: Orange County Developers Bank on the Growing Demand for Golf Courses," *Los Angeles Times*, May 12, 1991, sec. D, p. 1.

7. Joel Garreau, *Edge City: Life on the New Frontier* (Doubleday, 1991).

8. Interview with Marta Borsanyi, Robert Charles Lesser and Company, November 27, 1993.

9. Quoted in David Guterson, "Home, Safe Home," *Utne Reader*, March/April 1993, p. 62.

10. Ibid.

11. Site visit, March 1994.

12. Focus group session with public officials, Palm Springs, California, September 29, 1994.

13. Ibid.

14. Ibid.

Chapter Four

1. Robert A. M. Stern, ed., *The Anglo-American Suburb*, Architectural Design Profile (New York: St. Martin's Press, 1981).

2. *Town and Country*, "Wealth in America," report of a poll conducted by Roper Starch Worldwide in 1993 for *Town and Country* magazine, 1994.

3. Interview with Chuck Lennon, executive director of the Builders Association of South Florida, Miami Lakes, Florida, December 9, 1994.

4. Interview with Curt Wellwood, Curt Wellwood Homes, Dallas, Texas, November 29, 1994.

5. Quoted in John M. Glionna, "Hidden Hills Likes Its Politics Out of View," *Los Angeles Times*, April 11, 1994, sec. A, p. 1.

6. Quoted by Ina Jaffe, "Gated Communities Controversy in Los Angeles," *All Things Considered*, National Public Radio, August 11, 1992.

7. Quoted in Dianne Stallings, "Hernando County, with Its Reputation for Housing Bargains, Becoming a Prime Location for a Grand Style of House," *St. Petersburg Times,* October 4, 1987, p. H1.

8. Lorraine Mirabella, "Selling Security," *Baltimore Sun*, December 11, 1994, p. L1.

9. Charles Lesser and Co., "Flexexecutive: Redefining the American Dream," *Advisory*, Fall 1994.

10. Gary A. Clark, "City Boys Go West for Change: Conner, Bruno Join Forces in Development," *St. Louis Post-Dispatch*, June 25, 1989, p. 4.

11. Quoted in Jackie Ripley, "Nature's Way," *St. Petersburg Times*, July 21, 1991, p. 9.

12. Quoted in David Harpster, "Plans for Stagecoach Springs Bounce Along," *San Diego Union-Tribune*, February 1, 1994, p. B1.

13. Focus group session with Dallas public officials, November 29, 1994.

14. Doreen Heisler and Warren Klein, *Inside Look at Community Association Homeownership: Facts and Perceptions* (Alexandria, Va.: Community Associations Institute, 1996).

15. Focus group session with Dallas public officials, November 29, 1994.

Chapter Five

1. See Time/CNN Poll by Yankelovich Partners, Inc., reported in Jon D. Hull, "The State of the Union," *Time*, January 30, 1995, p. 63; Ronet Bachman, *Crime Victimization in City, Suburban, and Rural Areas* (Washington, D.C.: Bureau of Justice Statistics, U.S. Department of Justice, 1992); and Carol J. DeFrances and Steven K. Smith, *Crime and Neighborhoods* (Washington, D.C.: Bureau of Justice Statistics, U.S. Department of Justice, 1994), p. 2.

2. Bachman, *Crime Victimization* , p. 4.

3. Bureau of Justice Statistics, *National Crime Victimization Survey* (Washington, D.C.: U.S. Department of Justice, 1993).

4. Quoted in Gabriel Escobar and Patrice Gaines-Carter, "A Housing Complex Divided: Anti-Crime Fencing Angers Some Potomac Garden Residents," *Washington Post*, June 14, 1992, sec. A, p. 1.

5. Santiago O'Donnell, "More Than a Fence: 8-Foot Barrier Helped Cut Crime, Instill Hope at Potomac Gardens," *Washington Post*, December 10, 1992, sec. DC, p. 1.

6. Miles Corwin, "Low-Income Project Gets Chic Security," *Los Angeles Times*, March 15, 1992, sec. B, p. 1.

7. Oscar Newman, "Defensible Space: A New Physical Planning Tool for Urban Revitalization," *Journal of the American Planning Association,* vol. 61, no. 2 (Spring 1995), pp. 149–55.

8. Corwin, "Low-Income Project."

9. *Citizens against Gated Enclaves* v. *Whitley Heights Civic Association and the City of Los Angeles*, California State Court of Appeals, Harold J. (Fred) Woods, Judge, March 23, 1994.

10. Tom Lassiter, "Homeowners Explore Limiting Access," *Sun-Sentinel*, March 20, 1994, Broward ed., p. 5.

11. Russ Loar, "Gating of College Park West Proposed," *Los Angeles Times*, Orange County ed., sec. B, pp. 2–6.

12. Stephanie Simon, "Gate Debate Lingers at Posh Community," *Los Angeles Times*, January 3, 1995, sec. B, pp. 1–2.

13. Associated Press, "Life behind Barricades: The New U.S. Community," *St. Petersburg Times*, February 2, 1993, p. A1.

14. Kevin V. Johnson, "Chicago Suburb a Fortress against Crime," *USA Today*, July 6, 1995, p. 3A.

15. Mary Moore, "Part of Brentwood Allowed to Become Gated Community," *Los Angeles Times*, June 4, 1995, Westside ed., sec. J, p. 3.

16. Mary Moore, "Brentwood Road Bloc; Communities: Residents of Enclave Near the Getty Center Receive Tentative City Council Approval to Erect Gates," *Los Angeles Times*, May 18, 1995, sec. J, p. 3.

17. Bob Campbell, "Community Seeks to Close Gate on Crime," *St. Petersburg Times*, February 11, 1992, p. 1.

18. Walt Yost, "Council Pounds the Pavement: Franklin Villa Site of First 'Road Show,'" *Sacramento Bee*, August 26, 1993, p. N1; see also editorial, "Fenced in at Franklin Villa," *Sacramento Bee*, March 16, 1993, p. B6.

19. Diana Sugg, "Small Neighborhood under Siege: Hopes and Dreams Swept away by Wave of Drug Dealing, Gun Battles," *Sacramento Bee*, January 31, 1993, p. B1.

20. Quoted in Ina Jaffe, "Gated Communities Controversy in Los Angeles," *All Things Considered.* National Public Radio, August 11, 1992.

21. Oscar Newman, *Improving the Viability of Two Dayton Communities: Five Oaks and Dunbar Manor* (Great Neck, N.Y.: Institute for Community Design Analysis, 1992), p. 14.

22. Mitchell Owens, "Saving Neighborhoods One Gate at a Time," *New York Times*, August 25, 1994, sec. B, p. 1.

23. Interview with Christina Abrams, planner, Coconut Grove NET, City of Miami, December 7, 1994.

24. John Williams, "Blocked Off; U.S. Probes Houston's Street Closures for Racial Intent," *Chicago Tribune*, January 1, 1995, Real Estate section, p. 4.

25. Oscar Newman, *Community of Interest* (Garden City, N.Y.: Anchor Press/Doubleday, 1980), chapter 6.

26. Ibid.

27. Fort Lauderdale Police Department, Crime Prevention/Planning and Research Unit, *Street Closure Study*, September 20, 1990, p. 9.

28. Interview with Louis Wechsler, president of the homeowner association of South Coconut Grove, December 7, 1994.

Chapter Six

1. Time/CNN Poll by Yankelovich Partners, Inc., reported in Jon D. Hull, "The State of the Nation," *Time*, January 30, 1995, p. 63.

2. Cited in Miles Corwin, "Guns for Hire: A Growing Corps of Private Cops Is the First Line of Defense for Homes and Shops—but at a Price," *Los Angeles Times*, November 28, 1993, Magazine, p. 24.

3. Focus group session, Plano, Texas, November 28, 1994.

4. Oscar Newman, *Community of Interest* (Garden City, N.Y.: Anchor Press/Doubleday, 1980); Robert E. Park, Ernest W. Burgess, and Roderick D. McKenzie, *The City* (University of Chicago Press, 1925); Constance Perin, *Everything in Its Place: Social Order and Land Use in America* (Princeton University Press, 1977); Gerald D. Suttles, *The Social Construction of Communities* (University of Chicago Press, 1972).

5. Robert J. Dilger, *Neighborhood Politics: Residential Community Associations in American Governance* (New York University Press, 1992); Robert H. Nelson, "Private Neighborhoods: A New Direction for the Neighborhood Movement," in Charles C. Geisler and Frank J. Popper, eds., *Land Reform American Style* (Totowah, N.J.: Rowman and Allanheld, 1984).

6. It was not possible to make a direct comparison of gated and nongated communities. Although the CAI kindly appended our survey of gated communities to its survey of homeowner association membership, we were given access only to the raw data from our gated communities section. The CAI's published analysis of the data included no comparison between gated and nongated communities except the security perception data reported in the previous section.

7. Mark Baldassare and Georjeanna Wilson, "Overall 'Sense of Community' in a Suburban Region: The Effects of Localism, Privacy and Urbanization," Working Paper 1994-15 (Department of Urban and Regional Planning, University of California at Irvine, 1994), p. 9.

8. Carol J. Silverman and Stephen E. Barton, "Shared Premises: Community and Conflict in the Common Interest Development," in Stephen E. Barton and Carol J. Silverman, eds., *Common Interest Communities: Private Government and the Public Interest* (Institute of Governmental Studies Press, University of California at Berkeley, 1994); *Common Interest Homeowners' Association Management Study* (Sacramento: California Department of Real Estate, 1987); Dilger, *Neighborhood Politics*; Gregory S. Alexander, "Conditions of 'Voice': Passivity, Disappointment, and Democracy in Homeowner Associations," in Barton and Silverman, *Common Interest Communities*.

9. Marc Lacey, "Inside the Gates: A Naive Little Utopia," *Los Angeles Times*, June 16, 1991, sec. B, p. 3.

10. Amitai Etzioni, *The Spirit of Community: Rights, Responsibilities, and the Communitarian Agenda* (New York: Crown Publishers, 1993).

11. David M. Hummon, *Commonplaces: Community Ideology and Identity in American Culture* (Albany: State University of New York Press, 1990).

12. Robert N. Bellah and others, *Habits of the Heart: Individualism and Commitment in American Life* (Harper and Row, 1986), p. 37.

13. Ibid., p. 181.

14. Focus group session with realtors working in Blackhawk, California, September 28, 1994.

15. Newman, *Community of Interest*, p. 133.

16. Gregory S. Alexander, "Dilemmas of Group Autonomy: Residential Associations and Community," *Cornell Law Review*, vol. 75, no. 1 (1989), p. 61.

17. Daniel Kemmis, "Living Next to One Another," *Parabola*, Winter 1993.

18. Focus group session with public officials in Plano, Texas, November 28, 1994.

Chapter Seven

1. William W. Goldsmith and Edward J. Blakely, *Separate Societies: Poverty and Inequality in U.S. Cities* (Temple University Press, 1992).

2. Brad Edmundson, "Seven Generations," *American Demographics*, January 1995, p. 52.

3. Mike Davis, *City of Quartz: Excavating the Future in Los Angeles* (New York: Verso, 1990), p. 130.

4. Charles Lockwood, "Edge Cities on the Brink," *Wall Street Journal*, Wednesday, December 21, 1994, p. A18.

5. Anthony Downs, *New Visions for Metropolitan America* (Brookings and Lincoln Institute of Land Policy, 1994), p. 204.

6. Reynolds Farley and others, "Continued Racial Segregation in Detroit: 'Chocolate City, Vanilla Suburbs' Revisited," *Journal of Housing Research*, vol. 44, no. 1 (1993), pp. 1–38.

7. George Galster, "Black Suburbanization: Has It Changed the Relative Location of Races?" *Urban Affairs Quarterly*, vol. 26, no. 4 (June 1991), p. 622.

8. Douglas S. Massey and Nancy A. Denton, *American Apartheid: Segregation and the Making of the Underclass* (Harvard University Press, 1993), p. 69.

9. Greg Hinz, "Moving Violation," *Chicago*, March 1994, p. 21.

10. Massey and Denton, *American Apartheid*, p. 222.

11. Ibid.

12. Nancy Denton, "Are African Americans Still Hypersegregated?" in Rob-

ert Bullard, J. Eugene Grigsby, and Charles Lee, eds., *Residential Apartheid: The American Legacy* (Los Angeles: CAAS Publications, 1994), pp. 62, 74.

13. Massey and Denton, *American Apartheid*; George C. Galster and Sean P. Killen, "The Geography of Metropolitan Opportunity: A Reconnaissance and Conceptual Framework," *Housing Policy Debate,* vol. 6, no. 1 (1995), pp. 7–41.

14. Alan J. Abramson, Mitchell S. Tobin, and Matthew R. VanderGoot, "The Changing Geography of Metropolitan Opportunity: The Segregation of the Poor in U.S. Metropolitan Areas, 1970 to 1990," *Housing Policy Debate,* vol. 6, no. 1 (1995), pp. 45–72.

15. Claude S. Fischer and others, *Inequality by Design: Cracking the Bell Curve Myth* (Princeton University Press, 1996).

16. Dennis R. Judd, "The Rise of the New Walled Cities," in Helen Liggett and David C. Perry, eds., *Spatial Practices: Critical Explorations in Social/Spatial Theory* (Thousand Oaks, Calif.: Sage Publications, 1995), p. 161.

17. See Mark Baldassare, Annual Orange County Survey conducted by the University of California at Irvine, 1994; and Jon D. Hull, "The State of the Union," *Time*, January 30, 1995, p. 63.

18. Patrick T. Reardon, "Fears, Frustrations Set Off the Exodus," *Chicago Tribune*, November 29, 1993, p. 1.

19. Bureau of Justice Statistics, *National Crime Victimization Survey* (Washington, D.C.: U.S. Department of Justice, 1993).

20. Edward J. Blakely, "Shaping the American Dream: Land Use Choices for America's Future," Working Paper (Lincoln Institute of Land Policy, Cambridge, Massachusetts, 1993).

21. Gail George, "Immigrants Spur Appeals to the Feds and Crime Sends Tourists toward Calmer Climes," *Business Week*, September 19, 1994, p. 4.

22. William H. Frey, "Immigration and Internal Migration Flight from U.S. Metropolitan Areas: Toward a New Demographic Balkanization," *Urban Studies,* vol. 32, no. 4 (1995), pp. 733–57.

23. Dale Maharidge, "Walled Off," essay for publication in *Mother Jones Magazine*, n.d., 1995.

24. Galster and Killen, "Geography of Metropolitan Opportunity."

25. John Kain, "The Spatial Mismatch Hypothesis: Three Decades Later," *Housing Policy Debate,* vol. 6, no. 1 (1995), pp. 371–460.

26. William Julius Wilson, *The Truly Disadvantaged: The Inner City, the Underclass, and Public Policy* (University of Chicago Press, 1987), p. 60.

27. Associated Press, "Life behind Barricades: The New U.S. Community," *St. Petersburg Times*, February 2, 1993, p. A1.

28. Art Lawler, "Perot Group Project Has a Fast Start," *Dallas Morning News*, March 26, 1992, p. 1F.

29. Robert Bullard, J. Eugene Grigsby, and Charles Lee, *Residential Apartheid: The American Legacy* (Los Angeles: CAAS Publications, 1994).

30. Y. Rabin, "The Persistence of Racial Isolation: The Role of Government Action," Working Paper (Department of Urban Studies, Massachusetts Institute of Technology, 1991).

31. Quoted in Constance Perin, *Everything in Its Place: Social Order and Land Use in America* (Princeton University Press, 1977), p. 87.

32. See Jim Schwab, "Home, Safe Home?" *Zoning News*, American Planning Association, September 1993, p. 3.

33. Interview with city officials in Plano, Texas, November 28, 1994.

34. June Fletcher, "Behind Walls, Millions Seek Safe Havens," *Wall Street Journal*, February 2, 1996, p. B8.

35. Bennett Roth, "Barricading Streets Can't Cut Off Controversy," *Los Angeles Times*, January 31, 1994, sec. B, p. 1.

36. J. Linn Allen, "Today's Castles: Some Seek Refuge behind Walls, Gates," *Chicago Tribune*, May 12, 1990, Home Guide, Zone C, p. 1.

37. Focus group session with Dallas public officials, November 29, 1994.

38. Metropolitan Area Planning Department, "Report on Gated Subdivisions" (Wichita, Kansas, September 13, 1995), p. 6.

39. Minutes, Metropolitan Area Planning Commission, Wichita, Kansas, September 28, 1995.

40. Quoted in Stephanie Simon, "Thousand Oaks City Council to Vote on Enclave's Gate Plan," *Los Angeles Times*, April 27, 1993, sec. B, p. 1.

41. Quoted in Bob Campbell, "Subdivision Security Plan Is Critiqued," *St. Petersburg Times*, March 11, 1992, sec. 1, p. 1.

42. Quoted in Ina Jaffe, "Gated Communities Controversy in Los Angeles," *All Things Considered*. National Public Radio, August 11, 1992.

43. Quoted in Allen, "Today's Castles."

44. Mitchell Owens, "Saving Neighborhoods One Gate at a Time," *New York Times*, August 25, 1994, sec. B, p. 1.

Chapter Eight

1. See Oscar Newman, *Defensible Space; Crime Prevention through Urban Design* (Macmillan, 1972); and Jane Jacobs, *The Death and Life of Great American Cities* (Modern Library, 1993).

2. Oscar Newman, *Community of Interest* (Garden City, N.Y.: Anchor Press/Doubleday, 1980).

3. Gerda R. Wekerle and Carolyn Whitzman, *Safe Cities: Guidelines for Planning, Design, and Management* (New York: Van Nostrand Reinhold, 1995), p. 51.

4. Stephanie Mann with M. C. Blakeman, *Safe Homes: Safe Neighborhoods: Stopping Crime Where You Live* (Berkeley, Calif.: Nolo Press, 1993).

5. Lorraine Woellert, "Celebrating Diversity Makes Difference; Mount Pleasant Puts Riot, Polarity in Past-Tense View," *Washington Times*, May 24, 1993, p. B1.

6. Brenda Eubank, "A Closer Look at the Users of Woonerven," in Anne Vernez Moudon, *Public Streets for Public Use* (New York: Van Nostrand Reinhold, 1987).

7. John M. Fernandez, "Builder Brings Back the Neighborhood Street," *Planning*, June 1994, pp. 21–26.

8. Eubank, "A Closer Look"; Michael Southworth and Eran Ben-Joseph, "Regulated Streets: The Evolution of Standards for Suburban Residential Streets," Working Paper 593 (Institute of Urban and Regional Development, University of California at Berkeley, 1993).

9. Fernandez, "Builder Brings Back the Neighborhood Street."

10. Timothy Beatley and David J. Brower, "Sustainability Comes to Main Street," *Planning*, May 1993; and Sim Van der Ryn and Peter Calthorpe, eds., *Sustainable Communities: A New Design Synthesis for Cities, Suburbs and Towns* (San Francisco: Sierra Club Books, 1986).

11. John Hagan and Ruth D. Peterson, eds., *Crime and Inequality* (Stanford University Press, 1995).

12. Robert A. M. Stern, ed., *The Anglo-American Suburb*, Architectural Design Profile (New York: St. Martin's Press, 1981).

13. Philip Langdon, *A Better Place to Live: Reshaping the American Suburb* (University of Massachusetts Press, 1994).

14. Susan Handy, "Neo-traditional Development: The Debate," *Berkeley Planning Journal* (1991), pp. 135–44.

15. Peter Calthorpe, *The Next American Metropolis: Ecology, Community, and the American Dream* (Princeton, N.J.: Princeton Architectural Press, 1993), p. 37.

16. Mark Baldasarre, *Trouble in Paradise: The Suburban Transformation in America* (Columbia University Press, 1986), p. 144.

17. Anthony Downs, *New Visions for Metropolitan America* (Brookings and Lincoln Institute for Land Use Policy, 1994), p. 58.

18. BRIDGE Housing Corporation was created by a public-private partnership of the Bay Area Council and has produced mixed-income and mixed-use housing succesfully for more than a decade. BRIDGE is one of the top 100 builders of multifamily dwellings in the United States.

19. William W. Goldsmith and Edward J. Blakely, *Separate Societies: Poverty and Inequality in U.S. Cities* (Temple University Press, 1992).

20. Daniel Patrick Moynihan, *The Negro Family: The Case for National Action* (Washington, D.C.: U.S. Department of Labor, 1965).

21. John Gardner, former secretary of Health and Human Services, has written and spoken on the topic of community as the only meaningful mechanism for integrating the nation's rising tide of diversity. Amitai Etzioni has co-founded a journal, *The Responsive Community*, that focuses on building a new social ethic for community.

22. Michael Walzer, *Spheres of Justice: A Defense of Pluralism and Equality* (Basic Books, 1983), p. 2.

23. Downs, *New Visions for Metropolitan America*, p. 205.

24. Eric F. Goldman, *Rendezvous with Destiny* (New York: Vintage Books, 1958), p. 347; Roosevelt quoted on p. 346.

References

Abramson, Alan J., Mitchell S. Tobin, and Matthew R. VanderGoot. "The Changing Geography of Metropolitan Opportunity: The Segregation of the Poor in U.S. Metropolitan Areas, 1970 to 1990." *Housing Policy Debate* 6, no. 1 (1995): 45–72.

Alexander, Gregory S. "Conditions of 'Voice': Passivity, Disappointment, and Democracy in Homeowner Associations." In Stephen E. Barton and Carol J. Silverman, eds., *Common Interest Communities: Private Government and the Public Interest.* Institute of Governmental Studies Press, University of California at Berkeley, 1994.

———. "Dilemmas of Group Autonomy: Residential Associations and Community." *Cornell Law Review* 75, no. 1 (1989):1-61.

Anderson, Elijah. *Streetwise: Race, Class and Change in an Urban Community.* University of Chicago Press, 1990.

Baldassare, Mark. Orange County Annual Survey. Irvine, Calif., Program in Social Ecology and Public Policy Research, University of California, 1994.

———. *Trouble in Paradise: The Suburban Transformation in America.* Columbia University Press, 1986.

Baldassare, Mark, and Georjeanna Wilson. "Overall 'Sense of Community' in a Suburban Region: The Effects of Localism, Privacy and Urbanization."

194

Working Paper 1994-15. Department of Urban and Regional Planning, University of California at Irvine, 1994.

Barton, Stephen E., and Carol J. Silverman. "Common Interest Communities: Private Government and the Public Interest Revisited." In Stephen E. Barton and Carol J. Silverman, eds., *Common Interest Communities: Private Government and the Public Interest.* Berkeley: Institute of Governmental Studies Press, University of California at Berkeley, 1994.

————. *Common Interest Homeowners' Association Management Study.* Sacramento: California Department of Real Estate, 1987.

Barton, Stephen E., and Carol J. Silverman, eds. *Common Interest Communities: Private Government and the Public Interest.* Berkeley: Institute of Governmental Studies Press, University of California at Berkeley, 1994.

Beatley, Timothy, and David J. Brower. "Sustainability Comes to Main Street." *Planning,* May 1993.

Bellah, Robert N., and others. *Habits of the Heart: Individualism and Commitment in American Life.* Harper and Row, 1986.

Blakely, Edward J. "Shaping the American Dream: Land Use Choices for America's Future." Working Paper. Lincoln Institute of Land Policy, Cambridge, Mass., 1993.

Boddy, Trevor. "Underground and Overhead: Building the Analogous City." In Michael Sorkin, ed. *Variations on a Theme Park: The New American City and the End of Public Space.* New York: Hill and Wang, 1992.

Bowen, W. A. *Selected Statistics and Comments Concerning Poverty in California and the Nation.* Department of Geography, California State University, Northridge.

Bruegmann, Robert. "The Twenty-Three Percent Solution." *American Quarterly* 46, no. 1 (March 1994): 31–34.

Bullard, Robert, J. Eugene Grigsby, and Charles Lee, eds. *Residential Apartheid: The American Legacy.* Los Angeles: CAAS Publications, 1994.

Bureau of Justice Statistics. *National Crime Victimization Survey.* Washington, D.C.: U.S. Department of Justice, 1993.

————. *Rural, Suburban, and Inner City Victimization.* Washington, D.C.: U.S. Department of Justice, 1989.

Citizens against Gated Enclaves v. *Whitley Heights Civic Association and the City of Los Angeles.* California State Court of Appeals, Harold J. (Fred) Woods, Judge. March 23, 1994.

Calthorpe, Peter. *The Next American Metropolis: Ecology, Community, and the American Dream.* New York: Princeton Architectural Press, 1993.

Charles Lesser and Co. "Flexexecutive: Redefining the American Dream." *Advisory,* Fall 1994.

Chinitz, Ben. "A Framework for Speculating about Future Urban Growth Patterns in the United States." Lincoln Institute of Land Policy, Cambridge, Mass., 1991.

"Crime: Safer Streets, Yet Greater Fear." *Time*, January 20, 1995.

Danielson, Michael N. *The Politics of Exclusion*. Columbia University Press, 1976.

Davis, Mike. *City of Quartz: Excavating the Future in Los Angeles*. New York: Verso, 1990.

————. "Fortress Los Angeles: The Militarization of Urban Space." In Michael Sorkin, ed., *Variations on a Theme Park: The New American City and the End of Public Space*. New York: Hill and Wang, 1992.

Defrances, Carol J., and Steven K. Smith. Crime and Neighborhoods. Washington, D.C.: Bureau of Justice Statistics, U.S. Department of Justice, 1994.

Denton, Nancy. "Are African Americans Still Hypersegregated?" In Robert Bullard, J. Eugene Grigsby, and Charles Lee, eds., *Residential Apartheid: The American Legacy.* Los Angeles: CAAS Publications, 1994.

Dilger, Robert J. *Neighborhood Politics: Residential Community Associations in American Governance*. New York University Press, 1992.

Downs, Anthony. *New Visions for Metropolitan America*. Brookings and Lincoln Institute of Land Policy, 1994.

Edmundson, Brad. "Seven Generations." *American Demographics*, January 1995.

Etzioni, Amitai. *The Spirit of Community: Rights, Responsibilities, and the Communitarian Agenda*. New York: Crown Publishers, 1993.

Eubank, Brenda. "A Closer Look at the Users of Woonerven." In Anne Vernez Moudon, *Public Streets for Public Use*. New York: Van Nostrand Reinhold, 1987.

Farley, Reynolds and others. "Continued Racial Residential Segregation in Detroit: 'Chocolate City, Vanilla Suburbs' Revisited." *Journal of Housing Research* 4, no. 1 (1993): 1–38.

Fischer, Claude S. *To Dwell among Friends: Personal Networks in Town and City*. University of Chicago Press, 1982.

Fischer, Claude S. and others. *Inequality by Design: Cracking the Bell Curve Myth*. Princeton University Press, 1996.

Fishman, Robert. *Bourgeois Utopias: The Rise and Fall of Suburbia*. Basic Books, 1987.

Ft. Lauderdale (Fla.) Police Department, Crime Prevention/Planning and Research Unit. *Street Closure Study*. September 20, 1990.

————. "Four Income Families." *Money*, vol. 24, no. 2 (February 1995): 148–54.

Frey, William H. "Immigration and Internal Migration Flight from U.S. Metropolitan Areas: Toward a New Demographic Balkanization." *Urban Studies* 32, no. 4 (1995): 733–57.

Galster, George C. "Housing Discrimination and Urban Poverty of African-Americans." *Journal of Housing Research* 2, no. 2 (1991):87–122.

———. "Black Suburbanization: Has It Changed the Relative Location of Races?" *Urban Affairs Quarterly* 26, no. 4 (June 1991): 622.

Galster, George C., and Sean P. Killen. "The Geography of Metropolitan Opportunity: A Reconnaissance and Conceptual Framework." *Housing Policy Debate* 6, no. 1 (1995): 7–41.

Galster, George C., and Maris Mikelsons. "The Geography of Metropolitan Opportunity: A Case Study of Neighborhood Conditions Confronting Youth in Washington, D.C." *Housing Policy Debate* 6, no. 1 (1995): 73–103.

Gans, Herbert J. *The Levittowners: Ways of Life and Politics in a New Suburban Community*. Pantheon Books, 1967.

Garreau, Joel. *Edge City: Life on the New Frontier*. Doubleday, 1991.

Geisler, Charles C., and Frank J. Popper, eds. *Land Reform American Style*. Totowa, N.J.: Rowman and Allanheld, 1984.

George, Gail. "Immigrants Spur Appeals to the Feds and Crime Sends Tourists toward Calmer Climes." *Business Week*, September 19, 1994.

Glynn, Thomas J. "Psychological Sense of Community: Measurement and Application. *Human Relations* 34, no. 7 (1981): 789–818.

Goldman, Eric F. *Rendezvous with Destiny*.Vintage Books, 1958.

Goldsmith, William W., and Edward J. Blakely. *Separate Societies: Poverty and Inequality in U.S. Cities*. Temple University Press, 1992.

Guterson, David. "Home, Safe Home." *Utne Reader*, March/April 1993.

Hagan, John, and Ruth D. Peterson, eds. *Crime and Inequality*. Stanford University Press, 1995.

Handy, Susan. "Neo-traditional Development: The Debate." *Berkeley Planning Journal* 6 (1991): 135–44.

Heisler, Doreen, and Warren Klein. *Inside Look at Community Association Homeownership: Facts and Perceptions*. Alexandria, Va.: Community Associations Institute, 1996.

Hillery, George A., Jr. "Definitions of Community: Areas of Agreement." *Rural Sociology* 20 (June 1955): 118.

Hinz, Greg. "Moving Violation." *Chicago*, March 1994.

Hull, John. "The State of the Nation." *Time*, January 30, 1995.

Hummon, David M. *Commonplaces: Community Ideology and Identity in American Culture*. Albany: State University of New York Press, 1990.

Jackson, Kenneth. *Crabgrass Frontier: The Suburbanization of the United States*. New York: Oxford University Press, 1985.

Jacobs, Jane. *The Death and Life of Great American Cities*. Modern Library, 1993.

Janowitz, Morris. *Community Press in an Urban Setting: The Social Elements of Urbanism*. 2d ed. University of Chicago Press, 1967.

Judd, Dennis R. "The Rise of the New Walled Cities." In Helen Liggett and David C. Perry, eds., *Spatial Practices: Critical Explorations in Social/Spatial Theory*. Thousand Oaks, Calif.: Sage Publications, 1995.

Kain, John . "The Spatial Mismatch Hypothesis: Three Decades Later." *Housing Policy Debate* 6, no. 1 (1995): 371–460.

Kanter, Rosabeth Moss. *Commitment and Community: Communes and Utopias in Sociological Perspective*. Harvard University Press, 1972.

Keating, Dennis. *The Suburban Dilemma*. Temple University Press, 1994.

Kemmis, Daniel. "Living Next to One Another." *Parabola* (Winter 1993):6–11.

Kennedy, David J. "Residential Associations as State Actors: Regulating the Impact of Gated Communities on Nonmembers." *Yale Law Journal,* vol. 105, no. 3 (December 1995): 761–93.

Lakoff, Sanford A., with Daniel Rich, eds. *Private Government: Introductory Readings*. Glenview, Ill.: Scott, Foresman, 1973.

Landis, John. "Do Growth Controls Work? A New Assessment." Working Paper 547. Institute of Urban and Regional Development, University of California at Berkeley, 1991.

———. "The Future of America's Center Cities." University of California at Berkeley, 1988.

Langdon, Philip. *A Better Place to Live: Reshaping the American Suburb*. Amherst: University of Massachusetts Press, 1994.

Latham, Earl. "The Body Politic of the Corporation." In Edward S. Mason, ed., *The Corporation in Modern Society*. Harvard University Press, 1959.

Leinberger, Christopher B., and Charles Lockwood. "How Business Is Reshaping America." *Atlantic*, October 1986.

Leinberger, Christopher B. "Suburbia." Los Angeles, Calif.: Robert Charles Lesser and Co., 1993.

Liggett, Helen, and David C. Perry, eds. *Spatial Practices: Critical Explorations in Social/Spatial Theory*. Thousand Oaks, Calif.: Sage Publications, 1995.

Louv, Richard. *America II: The Book That Captures America in the Act of Creating the Future*. New York: Penguin, 1985.

McKenzie, Evan. *Privatopia: Homeowner Associations and the Rise of Residential Private Government*. Yale University Press, 1994.

Maharidge, Dale. "Walled Off." *Mother Jones Magazine*, vol. 19, no. 6 (Nov.–Dec. 1994): 26.

Mann, Stephanie, with M. C. Blakeman. *Safe Homes, Safe Neighborhoods: Stopping Crime Where You Live*. Berkeley, Calif.: Nolo Press, 1993.

Marcuse, Peter. "Not Chaos, but Walls: Postmodernism and the Partitioned City." In Sophie Watson and Katherin Gibson, eds., *Postmodern Cities and Spaces*. Oxford: Blackwell, 1995.

Massey, Douglas S., and Nancy A. Denton. *American Apartheid: Segregation and the Making of the Underclass.* Harvard University Press, 1993.

Metropolitan Area Planning Department. "Report on Gated Subdivisions." Wichita, Kansas, September 13, 1995.

Michelson, William. *Environmental Choice, Human Behavior, and Residential Satisfaction.* New York: Oxford University Press, 1977.

Nasar, Jack L., and David A. Julian. "The Psychological Sense of Community in the Neighborhood." *Journal of the American Planning Association,* vol. 6, no. 2 (Spring 1995): 178–84.

Nelson, Robert H. "Private Neighborhoods: A New Direction for the Neighborhood Movement." In Charles C. Geisler and Frank J. Popper, eds. *Land Reform American Style.* Totowah, N.J.: Rowman and Allanheld, 1984.

———. "The Privatization of Local Government: From Zoning to RCAs." In *Residential Community Associations: Private Governments in the Intergovernmental System?* Washington, D.C.: United States Advisory Commission on Intergovernmental Relations, 1989.

Newman, Oscar. *Community of Interest.* Garden City, N.Y.: Anchor Press/Doubleday, 1980.

———. *Defensible Space: Crime Prevention through Urban Design.* New York: Macmillan, 1972.

———. "Defensible Space: A New Physical Planning Tool for Urban Revitalization." *Journal of the American Planning Association* 61, no. 2 (Spring 1995): 149–55.

———. *Improving the Viability of Two Dayton Communities: Five Oaks and Dunbar Manor.* Great Neck, N.Y.: Institute for Community Design Analysis, 1992.

Nisbet, Robert A. *The Quest for Community.* New York: Oxford University Press, 1970.

Park, Robert E., Ernest W. Burgess, and Roderick D. McKenzie. *The City.* University of Chicago Press, 1925.

Parker, Rowland. *The Common Stream.* London: Granada Publishing, 1976.

Parrington, Vernon L. *The Colonial Mind: 1620–1800.* Harvest Books–Harcourt, Brace and Co., 1954.

Perin, Constance. *Everything in Its Place: Social Order and Land Use in America.* Princeton University Press, 1977.

Petersen, John E. "The Blossoming of Micro Governments." *Governing,* October 1994.

Rabin, Y. "The Persistence of Racial Isolation: The Role of Government Action." Working Paper. Department of Urban Studies, Massachusetts Institute of Technology, 1991.

Reich, Robert B. *The Work of Nations: Preparing Ourselves for 21st-Century Capitalism.* A. A. Knopf, 1991.

Sandefur, Gary D., and Marta Tienda, eds. *Divided Opportunities: Minorities, Poverty, and Social Policy*. New York: Plenum Press, 1988.

Scott, Stanley. "The Homes Association: Will 'Private Government' Serve the Public Interest?" *Public Affairs Report* 8, no. 1.

Sennett, Richard. *The Fall of Public Man*. W. W. Norton, 1992.

Sharpe, William, and Leonard Wallock. "Bold New City or Built-Up Burb?: Redefining Contemporary Suburbia." *American Quarterly* 46, no. 1 (March 1994): 1–30.

Sorkin, Michael, ed. *Variations on a Theme Park: Scenes from the New American City and the End of Public Space*. Hill and Wang, 1992.

Southworth, Michael, and Eran Ben-Joseph. "Regulated Streets: The Evolution of Standards for Suburban Residential Streets." Working Paper 593. Institute of Urban and Regional Development, University of California at Berkeley, 1993.

———. *Streets and the Shaping of Towns and Cities*. New York: McGraw-Hill, 1997.

Stern, Robert A. M., ed. *The Anglo-American Suburb*, Architectural Design Profile. New York: St. Martin's Press, 1981.

Sternlieb, George. "Charting the 1990s—Things Ain't What They Used to Be." *Journal of the American Planning Association* 56, no. 4 (1990): 492–96.

Suttles, Gerald. *The Social Construction of Communities*. University of Chicago Press, 1972.

Szymanski, Richard. "Can Changing Neighborhood Traffic Circulation Patterns Reduce Crime and Improve Personal Safety? A Quantitative Analysis of One Neighborhood's Efforts." Master's thesis, Department of City and Regional Planning, Florida Atlantic University, 1994.

Tönnies, Ferdinand. *Community and Society*. Translated and edited by Charles P. Loomis. 1887; New York: Harper & Row, 1963.

Town and Country. "Wealth in America." Hearst Corporation, 1994.

United States Advisory Commission on Intergovernmental Relations. *Residential Community Associations: Private Governments in the Intergovernmental System?* Washington, D.C.: USACIR, 1989.

U.S. Department of Labor, Office of Policy Planning and Research. *The Negro Family: The Case for National Action*. Washington, D.C.: 1965.

Van der Ryn, Sim, and Peter Calthorpe, eds. *Sustainable Communities: A New Design Synthesis for Cities, Suburbs, and Towns*. San Francisco: Sierra Club Books, 1986.

Vidal, Avis. "Reintegrating Disadvantaged Communities into the Fabric of Urban Life: The Role of Community Development." *Housing Policy Debate* 6, no. 1(1995): 169–230.

Vidich, Arthur J., and Joseph Bensman. *Small Town in Mass Society*. Princeton University Press, 1968.

Walzer, Michael. *Spheres of Justice: A Defense of Pluralism and Equality.* Basic Books, 1983.

Warren, Roland. *The Community in America.* Chicago: Rand McNally, 1978.

Webber, Melvin. "Order in Diversity: Community without Propinquity." In Lowdon Wingo Jr., ed. *Cities and Space: The Future Use of Urban Land,* essays from the fourth RFF Forum. Johns Hopkins University Press, 1963.

Weibe, Robert. *The Segmented Society: An Introduction to the Meaning of America.* New York: Oxford University, Press, 1975.

Weiss, Marc A. "Community Builders and Community Associations: The Role of Real Estate Developers in Private Residential Governance." In *Residential Community Associations: Private Governments in the Intergovernmental System.* Washington, D.C.: United States Advisory Commission on Intergovernmental Relations, 1989.

————. *The Rise of the Community Builders: The American Real Estate Industry and Urban Land Planning.* Columbia University Press, 1987.

Wekerle, Gerda R., and Carolyn Whitzman. *Safe Cities: Guidelines for Planning, Design, and Management.* New York: Van Nostrand Reinhold, 1995.

Wellman, Barry, and Barry Leighton. "Networks, Neighborhoods and Communities: Approaches to the Study of the Community Question." *Urban Affairs Quarterly* 14, no. 3 (1978): 363–90.

Wilson, William Julius. *The Truly Disadvantaged: The Inner City, the Underclass, and Public Policy.* University of Chicago Press, 1987.

Wingo, Lowdon Jr., ed. *Cities and Space: The Future Use of Urban Land,* essays from the fourth RFF Forum. Johns Hopkins University Press, 1963.

Wirth, Louis. "Urbanism as a Way of Life." *American Journal of Sociology* 44 (1938): 3–24.

Index

Abrams, Roy, 86–87, 98
Abramson, Alan, 150
Access, street patterns and, 8, 9
Alexander, Greg, 35, 138–39
Amado, Christine, 7
American Association of Retired
    People (AARP), 49
Anderson, Elijah, 36
Annexation, 14
Ascher, Charles Stern, 19
Athens Heights, Calif., 116–17
Atlas, Randall, 119

Baldassare, Mark, 103, 132, 150,
    172–73
Barricade perches, 10, 11, 42, 43–
    44, 114–20, 115
Barton, Stephen, 35

Beach, Jay, 118
Bellah, Robert, 36, 137
Ben-Joseph, Eran, 13
Bering, Ken, 57
Berkeley, California, 12
Better life, search for, 30
Blackhawk Country Club, Calif.,
    39, 57–63; community feeling,
    59–62; control in, 62; security
    issues in, 58–59; as small town, 63
Block parties, 166
Boddy, Trevor, 28
Boulevard Woods North, Fla., 108
Braemer Gardens, Calif., 108
Brentwood, Calif., 109–10
Briarwood, Calif., 135–36
Bureau, Jeff, 67
Butzlaff, Jeff, 69–70

CAGE. *See* Citizens against Gated
   Enclaves
CAI. *See* Community Associations
   Institute
Calthorpe, Peter, 40, 170; on gated
   communities, 171
Canyon Lake, Calif., 65–71, 66;
   children's view of, 68–69;
   Disaster Coordinating Commit-
   tee, 68; incorporates, 67; sustain-
   able community and, 169
Carlton Square, Calif., 135–36
CC&Rs. *See* Covenants, conditions,
   and restrictions
Celebration, Fla., 64
Charles Lesser and Company, 83
Chicago, Ill., 121; reasons for
   leaving, 150–51, 151
Cities: annexation strategies, 14;
   edge, 14, 58, 146; escape from,
   12–13; vs. suburbs, 172–73
Citizens against Gated Enclaves
   (CAGE), 106–07, 159
Citizens vs. taxpayers, 139–40
City perches, 42–43, 102–08, 103
Class (social), walls and, 4, 7, 75,
   76–81
Coach, community, 165
Coconut Grove, Fla., 121, 123
COGs (regional councils of govern-
   ment), 174
College Park West, Calif., 108
Color-creep, 150. *See also* Racial
   mixing
Common-interest communities, 136
Community, 71–73, 129–35, 140,
   176–77; building, 161–77;
   defensible space and, 122, 162–
   63; defining, 31–35, 33; home-
   owner associations and, 22–23;
   individualism vs., 136–37; lack

of, 89–90, 94, 96; perceived level
   of, 130, 131f, 132; regional spirit
   of, 173–74; satisfaction vs.
   participation, 59–62, 130; search
   for, 29–45; selling, 18–19; sense
   of, 2, 44–45; stimulating, 135–36;
   sustainable, 168–72
Community Associations Institute
   (CAI), 24, 38; community
   participation, 133–34; perceived
   level of community, 130, 131f,
   132; security survey, 127–28
Consumption, conspicuous, 4
Contract city model, 26
Control: architectural, 27–28;
   community and, 120–24; traffic,
   105, 106, 111
Conway, Martha, 6
Cottonwood Valley, Tex., 78–81,
   139
Covenants, conditions, and restrictions (CC&Rs), 20–23, 64, 79,
   113–14; acceptance of, 59, 62;
   changing, 94; community feeling
   and, 138–39; inflexibility of, 169;
   resistance to, 52, 85
CPTED. *See* Crime prevention
   through environmental design
Crime, 126–29; gates and, 126–28;
   perceived level, by security type,
   128; prevention, 162–66, 164t;
   rates, 100–101, 101; trends, Ft.
   Lauderdale, 123
Crime prevention through environmental design (CPTED), 122,
   162–66; tactics, 164
Cul-de-sac-ization, 144–45

Daley, Richard M., 121
Dana Point, Calif., 152
Defended community, 32

Defensible space, 122, 162–63
Democratic process, 138–39, 176–77
Denton, Nancy, 148–50
Desert Horizons, Calif., newsletter, 135
de Tocqueville, Alexis, 31, 137
Developer: community-building, 168–72; gating logic of, 15, 17–19; lifestyle communities, 46–47; prestige communities, 75; withdrawal, 85
Dilger, Robert, 35
Douglas, William O., 21
Downs, Anthony, 146–47, 173–74, 175
Duany, Andres, 40, 170

Economic systems, regional metropolitan, 172–75
Edge City, 58
Elderly, 17–18
Elitism, 137
Empty nesters, 18
Etzioni, Amitai, 136
Exclusion, 24–25, 26, 44–45, 79–80; community and, 138–39; racial segregation, 148, 153. *See also* Segregation
Executive communities, 42, 75, 90–98, 91

Family structure, declining, 175
Farley, Reynolds, 147–48
Fear, 1, 29–30, 99–101, 138; city flight and, 150–51, 151f, 155; community and, 120–24; Miami Shores, 118–19; protection of privilege and, 3; violent crime and, 5
Fischer, Claude, 150

Five Oaks, Ohio, 117
Fourier, Charles, 12
Franklin Villa, Calif., 116
Ft. Lauderdale, Fla., 122

Galster, George, 150
Gans, Herbert, 36
Garreau, Joel, 58
Gated communities, 1; community quality, 30–31; as defensible space, 163; democracy and, 3; distribution of, 5–8; evolution of, 3–10; as marketing device, 15–16; opposition to, 106–07, 157–59; segregation in, 147–48, 153; social issues/values of, 44t, 44–45, 144–60; summary, 140–43; sustainable community and, 169–70; typology of, 38–39
Gate guards, 28, 84, 88–89, 95–96
Gates: city neighborhood, 10; double, 111; exclusion and, 154; false sense of security with, 67–68, 87; keypad, 93; perceived crime rate and, 127, 127–28; regulation of, 156–57; vendor cards, 111
Gatewood, KS, 158–59
Gee, Jon, 67, 69
Gemienschaft, 31, 32
Geography of opportunity, 150
Gesellschaft, 31
Goldman, Eric, 176–77
Golf and leisure community, 39–40, 55–63; amenities, 45–46; Dove Canyon, Calif., 56
Governance system: HOAs as, 24; Mission Hills Country Club, 53–55; private, 19–20; problems with, 85–86; subdivision, 20–23. *See also* Contract city model

Government, regional councils of
(COGs), 174
Green Valley, Nev., 64–65
Grey Rock, Md., 83
Guards, private security, 30. *See
also* Gate guards

Habits of the Heart, 36
Hall, Marty, 67–68, 70–71
Hidden Hills, Calif., 27; low-income
housing and, 77
Hidden Valley, Calif., 108
Hillcrest/Newark, N.J., 117
Hilton Head Island, S.C., 39, 57
Homeowner associations (HOAs),
20–23, 30; characteristics, 24–27;
problems in, 23; survey, 178–79;
volunteer participation and, 34–
35, 135
Housing, equal access laws, 15
Houston, Tex., 121
Howard, Ebenezer, 19, 169
Hummon, David, 136

Image, crime and, 162–63
Immigration, 145–46, 152
Independence, Declaration of, 174
Indian Wells, Calif., 78
Individualism vs. community, 136–
37
Inequality, federal government and,
174
Interview methodology, 36
Irvine Company, 64, 169
Irvine Ranch, Calif., 40

Jacaranda Pointe, Fla., 92–94
Jackson, Kenneth, 14
Jacobs, Jane, 162
James, Sharpe, 117
Johnson, Samuel, 13

Jones, Ann, 157
Judd, Dennis, 150

Kain, John, 153
Kennedy, David, 24
Krumholz, Norman, 157

Lakewood contract city model, 25
Langdon, Phil, 170
Leisure World, 4, 39, 49, 50
Lesser, Charles, and Company, 83
Lifestyle communities, 38, 39–40,
40, 46–73, 50; community in, 71–
73; golf and leisure, 55–63;
leisure class, 47–49; retirement,
49–55; suburban new town, 63–71
Limited liability community, 32
Lincoln, Abraham, 177
Los Angeles, spatial segregation,
146–47, 147

McCulloch, Lexy, 158
McDowall, Bob, 105–06, 107–08
Magdalene Reserve, Fla., 92
Maharidge, Dale, 152
Manhattan, suburbs of, 14
Marblehead, Calif., 87–90, 139;
lack of community in, 89–90
Marcuse, Peter, 30
Marketing: community, 18–19;
gated communities, 15–16;
security, 18, 50–51
Massey, Douglas, 149–50
Mediation, institutional, 32
Meyers Company, 17
Miami Shores, Fla., 118–20, 157
Middle class, expansion of, 15, 46–
47
Minorities: growth of, 145; middle
class, 15
Mission Hills Country Club, 51–55;

political participation in, 52–53; self-government, 53–55

Mount Pleasant (Washington, D.C.), 166

Moynihan, Daniel Patrick, 175

Naming, subdivision, 14

Neighborhoods, 34; pride in, 165

Neighborhood Watch, 30, 163, 165

Neotraditionalism, 170–72

New Brighton, Long Island, 12

Newhall Land and Farming Company, 64

Newman, Oscar, 103, 122, 137–38, 162

New town, suburban, 39–40, 63–71; amenities, 46

New Visions for Metropolitan America, 173–74

No-growth policies, 154–55

Not-in-my-backyard (NIMBY) movements, 30

Olmsted, Frederick Law, 12

Opportunity, geography of, 150

Orange County, Calif., analysis, 16–17

Owens, Peter M., 9

Owens, Robert, 12

Palm Springs, Calif., 72

Park, Robert, 31–32

Participation, community, 132–33, 133; Mission Hills Country Club, 52–53; problem factors, 133–34, 134

Participatory consciousness, 35

Perches, 42–44; barricade, 114–20; city, 102–08, 103; suburb, 108–14, 109

Perin, Constance, 155

Petersen, John, 25

Place: power of, 35; pride of, 165

Plano, Tex., 156–57

Plater-Zyberk, Elizabeth, 170

Potomac Gardens (Washington, D.C.), 102

Poverty, 8, 146–47, 150; federal government and, 174

Prestige communities, 38, 40–42, 41, 74–98, 82; crime and community sense in, 97–98; executive, 90–96; rich and famous, 76–81; top-fifth, 81–90

Privacy: community vs., 2, 81, 120–21; equality and, 27–28; gate-monitors and, 85; HOAs and, 21, 35; suburban form and, 9

Privatization, 3, 8, 44–45, 176; Canyon Lake, Calif., 67

Property owners' association (POA), 67

Property tax rebates, 25

Property values, 16–17, 154

Public buildings and spaces, 9

Public housing, gating, 102

Racial mixing, 148, 152–53. *See also* Color-creep

Radburn, N.J., 20

Rancho Mirage, Calif., 72

Redwood Shores, Calif., 64

Regional metropolitan economic systems, 172–75

Reich, Robert, 24

Research approach, gated communities, 36–38

Responsibility, social, 22–23; gated communities and, 163

Retirement community, 4, 39, 49–55; amenities, 45. *See also* Mission Hills Country Club

Rich and famous enclaves, 41, 75, 76–81
Riverside, Ill., 13
Roosevelt, Franklin, 176
Rosemont, Ill., 109

Secession, civic, 25–27
Second-home complexes, 18, 48–49, 56–57
Security: community and, 120–24; marketing, 18, 50–51; porous border problems, 65, 68–69, 95–96; protection of privilege and, 3, 81; search for, 1, 15, 125–29, 126; two-tiered, 129; violent crime and, 5
Security industry: growth in, 126
Security zone communities, 38, 42–44, 43, 99–124; crime and community in, 120–24
Segregation: economic and social, 8, 146–48, 147, 153–55; high income and, 148–49; poor and blacks, 149t. See also Exclusion
Self-determination, local, 34–35
Services: civic secession and, 25–26; HOA provision of, 24; privatization of, 3, 8
Shared streets, 166–68
Silver Creek Valley Country Club, Calif., 65
Silverman, Carol, 35
Skidaway Island, The Landings at, 50–51
Small-town life, 63, 144
Social values, 44–45
Sociology, Chicago School of, 31–32
Southworth, Michael, 8, 9, 13
Stability, 44–45
Stagecoach Springs, Colo., 92
State actors, 24–25

Street: access patterns, 8, 9; closure, 10, 114–16, 121; grid system, 171; historic plan, 13t; integration, 166–68; open/closed streets, 122–23; slow, 167, 168
Suburban form, 9; nostalgia and, 144; roots of, 11–13; sociocultural aspects of, 14–15
Suburban new town. See New town, suburban
Suburban perches, 42, 43, 108–14, 109
Success, symbols of, 76
Sun City (retirement community developer), 39
Sunrise Palms, Calif., 110–14; community participation, 112–13; neighborliness, 113–14
Surveillance, natural, 162–63
Suttles, Gerald, 32

Target-hardeners, 162, 165
Tarrytown Heights, N.Y., 13
Taxpayers vs. citizens, 139–40
Territoriality, 162–63
Tönnies, Ferdinand, 31
Top-fifth developments, 41–42, 75, 81–90
Traffic calming, 166–68
Traffic control, 105, 111; good neighborhoods and, 166–68; public access and, 106
Turner, Frank, 129
Tuxedo Park, N.Y., 74

Underclass, 145–46; black, 149–50
University Place, Mo., 91–92
Urban community research, 36
Urbanism, new, 170–72

Vigilantism, HOAs and, 22

Walled cities, 1, 3–4
Walters, Rita, 157
Walzer, Michael, 175
Waters of Weeki Wachee, Fla., 82
Wekerle, Gerda, 165
Weston, Fla., 83–87; community in, 85, 87
Whitley Heights, Calif., 103, 104–08, 157

Whitley Heights Civic Association, 105–06; collapse of, 107–08
Whitzman, Carolyn, 165
Wilson, Georjeanna, 132
Wilson, William Julius, 36, 153
Wright, Frank Lloyd, 12

Yacht Haven, Calif., 95–96, 98

Zoning, exclusionary, 154–55